RUGBY
WORLD CUP™
JAPAN日本2019

THE OFFICIAL BOOK

First published by Carlton Books Limited in 2019

Carlton Books Limited
20 Mortimer Street
London W1T 3JW

A CIP catalogue record for this book is available from the British Library.

ISBN 978-1-78739-267-0

Author: Simon Collings
Project Director: Martin Corteel
Project Editor: Ross Hamilton
Project Art Editor: Luke Griffin
Designer: Darren Jordan
Production: Rachel Burgess

Printed in Dubai

All statistics correct at 25 March, 2019

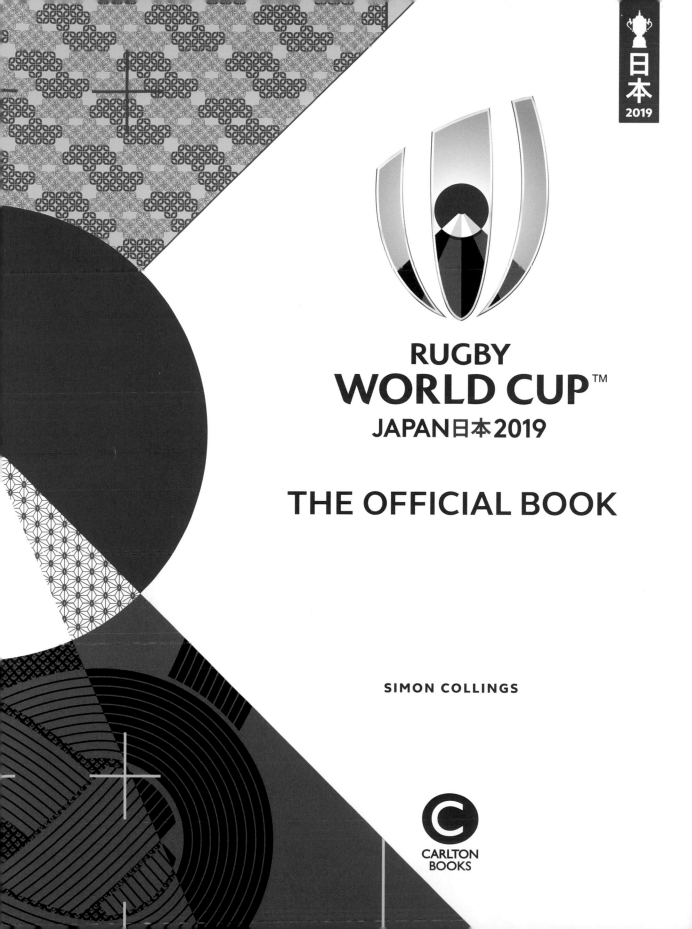

日本 2019

RUGBY
WORLD CUP™
JAPAN 日本 2019

THE OFFICIAL BOOK

SIMON COLLINGS

CARLTON
BOOKS

The International Rugby Football Board

The Webb Ellis Cup

Left: Teams will once again compete for the Webb Ellis Cup at Rugby World Cup 2019.

Following page: Japan promises to be one of the most scenic host nations ever.

CONTENTS

Introduction 8

Welcome to Japan 10
About Rugby World Cup 2019 12
Setting the scene for
    Rugby World Cup 2019 14
The rugby heritage of Japan 16
Match venues....................20
Magic moments:
    Serge of brilliance 24

The road to Japan..............26
How the teams qualified 28
World Rugby Rankings 32

Meet the teams....................34
Pool A: Ireland 36
Pool A: Scotland 38
Pool A: Japan 40
Pool A: Russia 42
Pool A: Samoa 44
Magic moments:
    Rugby unites a nation...............46
Pool B: New Zealand 48
Pool B: South Africa....................50
Pool B: Italy 52
Pool B: Namibia 54
Pool B: Canada............................56
Magic moments: Lomu announces
    himself by hitting England for
    four 58

Pool C: England............................60
Pool C: France 62
Pool C: Argentina.........................64
Pool C: USA 66
Pool C: Tonga................................68
Magic moments: Wilkinson kicks
    England to glory.........................70
Pool D: Australia 72
Pool D: Wales 74
Pool D: Georgia 76
Pool D: Fiji....................................78
Pool D: Uruguay 80
Magic moments: France fight back
    to stun New Zealand.................82

The stars to watch............84
Beauden Barrett 86
Jonathan Davies 87
Owen Farrell 88
Will Genia....................................89
Stuart Hogg 90
Michael Leitch............................. 91
Malcolm Marx 92
Sergio Parisse 93
Louis Picamoles 94
Semi Radradra 95
Nicolás Sánchez...........................96
Johnny Sexton..............................97
Magic moments: Carter is finally
    king of the world 98

Rugby World Cup
    history 100
Rugby World Cup 1987
    New Zealand / Australia 102
Rugby World Cup 1991
    UK, Ireland and France...........104
Rugby World Cup 1995
    South Africa.............................106
Rugby World Cup 1999
    Wales 108
Rugby World Cup 2003
    Australia....................................110
Rugby World Cup 2007
    France..112
Rugby World Cup 2011
    New Zealand 114
Rugby World Cup 2015
    England.....................................116
Magic moments: Japan's Brave
    Blossoms bloom to snare
    Springboks 118

Rugby World Cup
    facts and stats.................120
Rugby World Cup facts and stats:
    Teams 122
Rugby World Cup facts and stats:
    Players.......................................124
RWC 2019 tournament chart 126
Credits...128

INTRODUCTION

Since the inaugural tournament was held in New Zealand and Australia in 1987, Rugby World Cup has continued to grow. The 2019 edition promises to be bigger and better than ever, and for the first time an Asian country will play host. Japan is ready – and everyone is invited.

In the 32 years since its creation, Rugby World Cup has become one of the biggest sporting events on the planet. Rugby powerhouses such as England, New Zealand and South Africa have hosted the tournament in the past, but now it is ready to expand into new territories.

Japan are hosts of Rugby World Cup 2019, and that typifies how the game is growing all around the globe. Never before has the tournament been held in Asia and it promises to be an amazing spectacle. As soon as tickets went on priority sale in January 2018, the demand was there for all to see. Within seven months, 2.5 million applications had been made.

Supporters from all over the world are keen to travel to Japan and experience its unique culture while watching rugby's biggest stars go toe to toe. The country's brilliant transport system means fans can easily travel between the 12 stadia, taking in all the sights along the way.

Interest within Japan is high too, with support continuing to grow after the team's impressive three wins at Rugby World Cup 2015 – which included victory over two-time champions South Africa.

Japan's growth underlines how competitive the tournament promises to be and there will be plenty of teams fighting to lift the Webb Ellis Cup on 2 November in Yokohama.

New Zealand are hoping to win an unprecedented third Rugby World Cup in a row, but they will not have things all their own way.

Ireland's progress under Joe Schmidt makes them serious contenders, while a resurgent South Africa cannot be overlooked. The likes of Australia, England, France and Wales cannot be written off either.

All in all, an exciting tournament lies ahead and *Rugby World Cup 2019™, Japan: The Official Guide* has all the information a fan could need.

Below: Beauden Barrett scores for New Zealand during the final of Rugby World Cup 2015.

Opposite: The action at Rugby World Cup is always spectacular.

RUGBY WORLD CUP™
JAPAN日本2019

WELCOME TO JAPAN

Rugby World Cup 2019 promises to be a tournament like no other as an Asian country hosts the competition for the first time. Since the first Rugby World Cup in New Zealand and Australia in 1987, the sport has developed massively, and now it is Japan's turn to put on a memorable show. Watching in stunning stadia across the country, fans can expect an experience they will never forget.

Right: Japan players celebrate after their incredible victory over South Africa in Brighton at Rugby World Cup 2015.

ABOUT RUGBY WORLD CUP 2019™

The ninth edition of Rugby World Cup promises to be a spectacle like no other. Never before has the tournament been held in Asia, and Japan is ready to put on an incredible show. An unprecedented demand for tickets, combined with huge economic benefits and the prospect of growing the game in new countries, means that excitement is building ahead of what promises to be the sporting highlight of 2019.

The prospect of a Rugby World Cup in Japan has captured the imagination of fans everywhere. With a unique culture, bustling urban centres and stunning countryside, this is a nation famous the world over for its hospitality.

When Japan won the right to host Rugby World Cup 2019 back in 2009, the then president of the Japan Rugby Football Union (JRFU) Yoshirō Mori was a very happy man.

"The God of rugby smiled on us today," he said. "Japan has much to offer the Rugby World Cup. We have a superb transport system, strong infrastructure and world-class stadiums.

"I am filled with emotion to be a part of this historic day for Japan and for rugby around the world.

"We are honoured to welcome the global rugby family to our country and for the first time ever to Asia."

The organising committee for the tournament has ambitious targets as they try to put on a show that will live long in the memory.

As with any major sporting event, ticket sales play a major part and the demand for Rugby World Cup 2019 has been unprecedented. Organisers were expecting to sell 1.8 million tickets for the tournament when priority applications began in January

Above: The country's incredible transport network means fans will be able to travel all over Japan during the tournament.

Above: Japan's rugby fan base was boosted hugely after the team's showing at the last tournament in England.

2018. By July, they had received 2.5 million applications.

Around 400,000 visitors are predicted to travel to Japan for the 48 matches, with many keen to take in the 12 stadia located across the country.

Domestically, there has been a huge growth in the interest of the game too. That has partly been born out of Japan's strong showing at Rugby World Cup 2015, where they defeated two-time world champions South Africa in their opening match.

Their next match with Scotland drew TV viewing figures of 20 million, while the following encounter with Samoa peaked at 25 million. That was the biggest domestic audience ever for a Rugby World Cup match in Japan, and interest has grown from there.

Indeed, research by Nielsen in June 2018 estimated there were 14.9 million rugby supporters in Japan – a fan base that has increased by 20 per cent since the national team's heroics at Rugby World Cup 2015.

The tournament is predicted to bring a huge economic boost to Japan too, and again this could well be on a scale like never before. An economic impact study by Ernst & Young revealed in March 2018 that Rugby World Cup 2019 is set to deliver nearly ¥216.6 billion (£1.47 billion) of added value into the Japanese economy. The study estimates that the tournament will generate a total output of around ¥437.2 billion (£2.97 billion), underscoring the significant value in being the host nation.

Crucially that money will help ensure a long-lasting legacy is sustained from Rugby World Cup 2019, Japan.

Part of the idea behind the tournament going to Japan was that it would allow the game to grow in new areas. World Rugby is always keen to grow the family, and the sport is now blossoming in Asia. As part of the legacy of Rugby World Cup 2019, World Rugby, together with Asia Rugby, JR 2019 and JRFU,

set the bold target of reaching one million new players by 2020 across the continent – in line with the Impact Beyond 2019 strategy. This was achieved in December 2018.

"The World Rugby Council selected Japan as hosts because it presented a huge opportunity to grow the sport in Asia," said Tournament Director Alan Gilpin.

"The Impact Beyond 2019 legacy programme is shaping up to deliver a strong and sustainable hosting legacy for Asia."

In Japan, work has been carried out to ensure Rugby World Cup 2019 proves to be a springboard for the country. The Japan Rugby Football Union, together with the 12 host city unions, governments and rugby schools, have been running rugby introduction days for children new to the game, and in April 2018 alone they staged 100 such events.

The Future Plan has a key role to play in this and the idea is to have at least 200,000 active participants at all levels in Japan.

SETTING THE SCENE FOR RUGBY WORLD CUP 2019™

The growing interest in Asia ahead of Rugby World Cup 2019 was witnessed in November 2017 when the Webb Ellis Cup – rugby's most coveted prize – set off on an international Trophy Tour.

Leaving the World Rugby Hall of Fame in Rugby, England, the birthplace of the sport, the Webb Ellis Cup found new friends and fans as it made its way across 18 countries.

The Trophy Tour spread the word of the game far and wide by making visits to both established and emerging rugby nations, including China, the Philippines, Malaysia, Pakistan and Nepal. Records were broken along the way. In India, 15,000 school children in Bhubaneswar gathered to see the Webb Ellis Cup – the largest attendance at a stand-alone event since the Trophy Tour was introduced in 2014.

As with any major sporting event, volunteers will play a key role in Japan for Rugby World Cup 2019. At the previous tournament in England, volunteers were instrumental in ensuring the smooth running of the competition, and the plan remains the same this time around.

The Japan Rugby 2019 organising committee launched the programme "Team No-Side" to generate 10,000 volunteers. They will connect with fans, create unforgettable experiences and deliver an exceptional Rugby World Cup.

"The volunteers were at the heart of a very special Rugby World Cup 2015 and were certainly a highlight for fans and teams – they were the face of a tournament that had a superb carnival atmosphere," said World Rugby Chairman Bill Beaumont.

"Japan is famous for its hospitality and I am sure that 'Team No-Side' will play a key role in ensuring a memorable experience for all who attend Japan 2019."

Left: As part of a memorable Trophy Tour, the Webb Ellis Cup visited 18 countries across the globe to help promote the game.

Opposite: Just as they did at Rugby World Cup 2015, volunteers will play a big role in Japan.

KNOW THE GAME

POOL PHASE

The tournament's 20 nations have been drawn into four pools of five teams. Each team will play the other teams in its pool on a round-robin basis. The following number of points will be awarded for each match:

Win: 4 points
Draw: 2 points
Loss: 0 points
4 or more tries scored: 1 point
Loss by 7 points or fewer: 1 point

At the completion of the pool phase, the teams in a pool are ranked one to five based on their cumulative match points and identified respectively as winners, runner-up, third, fourth and fifth. The winner and runner-up in each pool qualify for the quarter-finals. The top three teams of each pool will also earn automatic qualification to Rugby World Cup 2023.

If two or more teams are level on match points at the completion of the pool phase, the following criteria shall be used in the following order until one of the teams can be determined as the higher ranked:

- The winner of the match between the two tied teams shall be ranked higher.
- The team that has the best difference between points for and points against during all its pool matches shall be ranked higher.
- The team that has the best difference between tries scored for and tries scored against during all its pool matches shall be ranked higher.
- The team who has scored the most points in all its pool matches shall be ranked higher.
- The team who has scored the most tries in all its pool matches shall be ranked higher.
- Should the tie be unresolved at the conclusion of all above steps, the rankings, as per the updated official World Rugby Rankings on 14 October, 2019, shall determine the higher ranked team.

KNOCKOUT MATCHES

If teams are tied at full-time, the winner shall be determined through the following sequential criteria:

Extra-time – following an interval of five minutes, extra-time of 10 minutes each way (with an interval of five minutes) shall be played in full.

Sudden death – if the scores are tied at the conclusion of extra-time, and following an interval of five minutes, then a further extra-time of 10 minutes maximum shall be played. During this period the first team to score any points shall be declared the winner.

Kicking competition – if after the sudden death period no winner can be declared, a kicking competition will be organised between the two teams. The winner of that competition shall be declared the winner of the match.

QUARTER-FINALS

The top two teams from each pool will progress to the last eight, and the quarter-final line-ups will be determined in the following way:
QF1: Winner of Pool C v Runner-up Pool D
QF2: Winner of Pool B v Runner-up Pool A
QF3: Winner of Pool D v Runner-up Pool C
QF4: Winner of Pool A v Runner-up Pool B

SEMI-FINALS

The semi-final line-ups will be decided in the following manner:
SF1: Winner QF1 v Winner QF2
SF2: Winner QF3 v Winner QF4

BRONZE FINAL

This match will be contested between the two losing semi-finalists.

THE FINAL

This match will be contested between the two winning semi-finalists.

THE RUGBY HERITAGE OF JAPAN

Rugby was first played in Japan more than 100 years ago. Since then, the sport has grown in popularity and the country is now ready to take centre stage as it prepares to host Rugby World Cup 2019.

To discover the first instance of rugby being played in Japan, you have to go all the way back to the 19th century.

In January 1866, *The Japan Times* reported the founding of the Yokohama Foot Ball Club. This was no simple matter back in those times when, unlike today, matches consisted of two teams of 20 players.

Even so, rugby left its first footprints in Yokohama, which had been a small fishing village just decades earlier. This was largely down to the great number of British soldiers stationed in the region at the time. Around 1,000 soldiers had been sent to Yokohama in 1864 following the Namamugi Incident two years earlier. Many of the officers stationed there came from rugby-playing schools, which had adopted the sport

following its birth in 1823 and they introduced the game to the people of Japan.

Legend has it that William Webb Ellis sparked the creation of the game back then by picking the ball up during a football match at Rugby School and running forward.

In that moment, rugby was born, and its spread through the English public school system led to it reaching Japanese shores.

By the start of 1868 one of Rugby School's alumni, George Hamilton, had arrived in the country, and he now became captain of the Yokohama Foot Ball Club. Along with others stationed out there, he helped drive the game's growth, and by the 1870s they were paying Yokohama Cricket Club to use their ground

during the rugby season.

At this time, the sport could be a difficult one to pick up for beginners because the rules differed from school to school. For that reason clubs, such as the one in Yokohama, had a committee to determine exactly what the rules would be. Matches were often played within clubs, with various criteria used to split the two teams up. Indeed, records from the time highlight a match-up between the "Talls" and "Shorts".

After establishing itself in Yokohama, rugby began to sweep the rest of Japan from 1899 onwards. Specifically, Keio University was the nucleus for the growth of rugby, thanks largely to the work of Professor Edward Bramwell Clarke

Left: Edward Bramwell Clarke (left) and Ginnosuke Tanaka were key to the early growth of rugby in Japan.

Opposite: Japan players line up for the national anthem at Rugby World Cup 2015.

and Ginnosuke Tanaka. Together the pair, who were both graduates of Cambridge University, taught rugby to the students at Keio. Clarke was particularly key in driving the game forward, playing alongside his students.

For him, it was an easy way to occupy his students who, he claimed at the time, "seemed to have nothing to occupy them out of doors in the after-summer and after-winter days. Winter baseball had not yet come in, and the young fellows loitered around, wasting the hours and the lovely outdoor weather."

That was certainly no longer the case once Clarke and Tanaka got their way, and within years they were breaking down racial and social barriers to play a match against the "Yokohama Foreigners" in 1901. Keio University lost 35-5, with Clarke converting a try scored by one of his students, but already rugby was demonstrating its ability to break down barriers.

By the 1920s, such was rugby's growth that universities were playing matches against each other. Rivalries that still exist today, such as the one between Keio and Waseda, were born and the National High School Rugby tournament was created.

The sport was booming and its popularity soared. Some 1,500 clubs had been established, while there were also 60,000 players registered. Even countries such as Ireland, Scotland and Wales could not match those numbers.

In 1926 another huge step was taken with the formation of the Japan Rugby Football Union (JRFU). The governing body set out on expanding the game even further and encouraged universities to go on tours.

Waseda University took up the flame and headed to Australia for three matches. The team returned having lost all their matches, but it was still a hugely significant step forward as the prospect of a Japanese national team began to become a reality.

As the popularity of rugby grew in Japan, a representative team toured British Columbia in Canada in 1930. They earned a 3-3 draw with Vancouver, but it was two years later that the real landmark moment came.

In 1932 Japan played their first-ever test match as Canada travelled to the country. The Canadian government, eager to strengthen trade links, financed the tour. Canada may have prospered economically from the trip,

but on the pitch there was only one winner: Japan won both tests.

The first encounter in Osaka proved to be a tight match as Japan claimed a 9-8 victory. However, the second contest 11 days later in Tokyo was a different story, and in front of a crowd of 35,000, the hosts won 38-5.

The school scene was still thriving, and an Australian Universities side toured Japan in 1934, with crowds of 20,000 flocking to watch them in action. They lost 14-9 to Japan and, two years later, Japan were held to a 9-9 draw by a visiting New Zealand Universities team.

The outbreak of the Second World War halted the progress of rugby in Japan and, for that matter, around the globe. Matches still took place in Japan until around 1943, but by then so many players had lost their lives. There was the impact too of the Japanese military seizing control of pitches.

When peace returned in 1945, so did rugby. The sport had an unexpected boom upon its comeback as schools in Kyoto began to play it again in September. Before long, others were following suit.

The appetite for rugby was clear for all to see and businesses soon began to realise the immense value

it would have on their staff. Kobe Steel had already encouraged its workers to take up the game and the likes of Ricoh and Toshiba followed their lead. By 1949, there were enough company sides to begin a national championship. To this day, businesses still have a huge influence on club rugby in Japan as shown by the teams in the modern-day Top League.

The university scene was also resurrected following the Second World War. Indeed, both Cambridge and Oxford toured Japan in the 1950s, while domestically crowds of 50,000 would turn out on an annual basis for the crunch match between Meiji and Waseda.

The National High School Rugby tournament grew in popularity too and was becoming one of the most important competitions in the whole of Japan.

More than 30 years after their historic win over Canada, the national team earned another landmark result in 1968. This time it was a 23-19 victory over the touring Junior All Blacks, and heading into the 1970s the game's growth was arguably stronger than ever in Japan.

In 1971 they welcomed England for two tests. Japan lost the first encounter 27-19, while the rematch was even closer as defeat came by the narrow margin of 6-3. It was an impressive performance by the hosts, who were playing a nation celebrating the centenary of their RFU.

Two years later, Japan headed to Wales, England and France. They won two of their 11 matches – against Western Counties (Wales) and a French Regional XV. A 62-14 defeat to Wales was part of Japan's tour, but when they returned in 1983 it was a different story. Once again they took on Wales at Cardiff Arms Park, but this time they were only narrowly beaten, 29-24.

Results like that gave Japan optimism as they prepared to take part in the inaugural Rugby World Cup four years later. However, they lost all three of their pool matches in Australia and New Zealand, which highlighted how much work was still to be done.

Four years later, Japan won their first-ever Rugby World Cup match, beating Zimbabwe 52-8 in Belfast.

For the next five tournaments, though, Japan failed to record a victory and managed only two draws.

It meant they headed to Rugby World Cup 2015 with minimal expectations from outside the country. However, coached by Eddie Jones, Japan pulled off one of the greatest shocks in rugby history by defeating two-time world champions South Africa 34-32 with a last-minute try.

They added two more wins, over Samoa and the USA, to finish third in Pool B – narrowly missing out on a place in the quarter-finals.

Japan had now shown their rugby potential to the world and the country's love of the game had grown even more.

Below: Japan claimed their first-ever Rugby World Cup win by defeating Zimbabwe in Belfast in 1991.

Right: Japan pulled off arguably the biggest shock in rugby history by defeating two-time Rugby World Cup champions South Africa in 2015.

MATCH VENUES

Twelve venues across as many cities have been chosen to host the 48 matches that will make up Rugby World Cup 2019. The tournament will span the length of Japan and provide supporters with an opportunity to visit the whole country. A mixture of new and existing stadia promises to give fans a different experience at each venue.

Fukuoka Hakatanomori Stadium
Fukuoka Prefecture, Fukuoka City

Kobe Misaki Stadium
Kobe City

City of Toyota Stadium
Aichi Prefecture, Toyota City

Kumagaya Rugby Stadium
Saitama Prefecture, Kumagaya City

Sapporo Dome
Sapporo City

Kamaishi Recovery Memorial Stadium
Iwate Prefecture, Kamaishi City

Shizuoka Stadium Ecopa
Shizuoka Prefecture

Tokyo Stadium
Tokyo Metropolitan

Kumamoto Stadium
Kumamoto Prefecture, Kumamoto City

Oita Stadium
Oita Prefecture

Hanazono Rugby Stadium
Osaka Prefecture, Higashiosaka City

International Stadium Yokohama
Kanagawa Prefecture, Yokohama City

The story of host city Kamaishi is one of the most inspiring at Rugby World Cup 2019. Back in 2011, the Great East Japan Earthquake and the tsunami that followed devastated the area. Rugby played a key role at the time by helping to bring a sense of normality back to life. The venue is the only newly built stadium of the tournament and pays tribute to the role played by rugby in bringing the community together.

Sapporo Dome

Capacity: 41,410
Matches hosted:
Australia v Fiji (D, 21 Sep)
England v Tonga (C, 22 Sep)

Constructed in 2001, the Sapporo Dome was one of the venues for the 2002 FIFA World Cup, which was hosted by Japan and South Korea. Now the venue is ready to add rugby to its list of sports. The Sapporo Dome is currently home of the baseball team Hokkaido Nippon-Ham Fighters and the football side Hokkaido Consadole Sapporo, but it has been used for other major events. It was the venue for the opening ceremony of the 2017 Asian Winter Games, just as it was for the FIS Nordic World Ski Championships back in 2007. The Sapporo Dome has two different surfaces, one made of artificial turf and the other grass, making it incredibly versatile.

Kamaishi Recovery Memorial Stadium

Capacity: 16,020
Matches hosted:
Fiji v Uruguay (D, 25 Sep)
Namibia v Canada (B, 13 Oct)

Tokyo Stadium

Capacity: 49,970
Matches hosted:
Japan v Russia (A, 20 Sep)
France v Argentina (C, 21 Sep)
Australia v Wales (D, 29 Sep)
England v Argentina (C, 5 Oct)
New Zealand v Namibia (B, 6 Oct)
Quarter-final 2 (19 Oct)
Quarter-final 4 (20 Oct)
Bronze final (1 Nov)

Usually the home of football clubs FC Tokyo and Tokyo Verdy, the Tokyo Stadium has a big role to play at Rugby World Cup 2019. The venue will host the opening ceremony as well as the first match of the tournament. In total, eight matches are scheduled to take place there, which is more than any other stadium. The venue is no stranger to hosting big events and has staged American Football and rugby in the past. Away from sport, the Tokyo Stadium has even hosted flea markets. It also played a vital role in the aftermath of the 2011 Tohoku earthquake and tsunami that struck Japan, when the stadium opened its doors to act as a shelter for survivors.

Above: The Sapporo Dome has hosted both summer and winter sports in the past.

Left: The Kamaishi Recovery Memorial Stadium is one of the most significant venues of Rugby World Cup 2019.

Above: In 2019, the International Stadium Yokohama will add Rugby World Cup to its CV.

Built as one of the venues for the FIFA World Cup in 2002, the Shizuoka Stadium Ecopa is ready to open its doors to rugby. Primarily used for football, the venue hosts J-League team Júbilo Iwata's more high-profile matches – such as the Shizuoka Derby. Fully equipped to stage track and field too, the stadium hosted the 58th National Sports Festival of Japan in 2003.

City of Toyota Stadium

Capacity: 45,000
Matches hosted:
Wales v Georgia (D, 23 Sep)
South Africa v Namibia (B, 28 Sep)
Japan v Samoa (A, 5 Oct)
New Zealand v Italy (B, 12 Oct)

With a stunning retractable roof that folds away like an accordion, the City of Toyota Stadium is one venue not to be missed at Rugby World Cup 2019. Its unique architecture helps create a great atmosphere, and Japan's match with Samoa promises to be a particular highlight.

Hanazono Rugby Stadium

Capacity: 24,100
Matches hosted:
Italy v Namibia (B, 22 Sep)
Argentina v Tonga (C, 28 Sep)
Georgia v Fiji (D, 3 Oct)
USA v Tonga (C, 13 Oct)

Built in 1929, the Hanazono Rugby Stadium is Japan's oldest dedicated rugby venue. It has a rich history, with the venue staging rugby matches across all ages and levels, from high school to professional matches. A hotbed for rugby, it stages Japan's National High School Rugby Tournament every year, drawing teams from all over the country.

International Stadium Yokohama

Capacity: 72,327
Matches hosted:
New Zealand v South Africa
  (B, 21 Sep)
Ireland v Scotland (A, 22 Sep)
England v France (C, 12 Oct)
Japan v Scotland (A, 13 Oct)
Semi-final 1 (26 Oct)
Semi-final 2 (27 Oct)
Final (2 Nov)

After hosting the football World Cup final in 2002, the International Stadium Yokohama is now set to stage the final of Rugby World Cup 2019. Boasting a capacity of more than 70,000, the stadium is the biggest at the tournament in Japan. In total, seven matches will take place there and it promises to provide a unique atmosphere for players and fans. The venue regularly hosts the FIFA Club World Cup final, but has also been used for American Football, athletics and rugby over the years. Music concerts are often held at the stadium too, with attendances occasionally reaching around 140,000.

Kumagaya Rugby Stadium

Capacity: 24,000
Matches hosted:
Russia v Samoa (A, 24 Sep)
Georgia v Uruguay (D, 29 Sep)
Argentina v USA (C, 9 Oct)

Constructed in 1991, the Kumagaya Rugby Stadium has been renovated as it prepares to host three matches at Rugby World Cup 2019. The venue is famous for its close ties to rugby and is often referred to as Japanese rugby's "hallowed ground of the East". Kumagaya's love of rugby makes it a perfect host city and it promises an unforgettable experience for fans.

Shizuoka Stadium Ecopa

Capacity: 50,889
Matches hosted:
Japan v Ireland (A, 28 Sep)
South Africa v Italy (B, 4 Oct)
Scotland v Russia (A, 9 Oct)
Australia v Georgia (D, 11 Oct)

Kobe Misaki Stadium

Capacity: 30,132
Matches hosted:
England v USA (C, 26 Sep)
Scotland v Samoa (A, 30 Sep)
Ireland v Russia (A, 3 Oct)
South Africa v Canada (B, 8 Oct)

Home of football club Vissel Kobe and rugby side Kobelco Steelers, the Kobe Misaki Stadium promises to provide fans with a unique atmosphere. The minimum length from the stand to the pitch is only six metres, which gives supporters the opportunity to see their favourite players up close.

Above: Rugby supporters will be impressed with the unique architecture of the Ōita Stadium.

Ōita Stadium

Capacity: 40,000
Matches hosted:
New Zealand v Canada (B, 2 Oct)
Australia v Uruguay (D, 5 Oct)
Wales v Fiji (D, 9 Oct)
Quarter-final 1 (19 Oct)
Quarter-final 3 (20 Oct)

Designed by Japanese architect Kisho Kurokawa, the Ōita Stadium opened in 2001 ahead of the FIFA World Cup the following year. The venue has the biggest retractable roof in Japan and has been nicknamed the "Big Eye" due to its resemblance to a winking eye.

Kumamoto Stadium

Capacity: 30,000
Matches hosted:
France v Tonga (C, 6 Oct)
Wales v Uruguay (D, 13 Oct)

With its eye-catching winged design, the Kumamoto Stadium is another example of the impressive architecture on show at Rugby World Cup 2019. The venue is mainly used for football matches, but it is no stranger to staging rugby having hosted Japan's Top League matches.

Fukuoka Hakatanomori Stadium

Capacity: 20,049
Matches hosted:
Italy v Canada (B, 26 Sep)
France v USA (C, 2 Oct)
Ireland v Samoa (A, 12 Oct)

Surrounded by forests in the centre of Fukuoka City, the area around Fukuoka Hakatanomori Stadium is a hub for all sports. Athletics, archery, baseball and tennis all take place there – but it is the rugby stadium that takes centre stage. With a capacity of over 20,000, it has been used for Pacific Nations Cup and Asian Five Nations matches in the past.

Above: Kumamoto Stadium has hosted both football and Top League rugby in the past.

SERGE OF BRILLIANCE

13 June, 1987: Concord Oval, Sydney

Over the years, France have developed a reputation for pulling off the sublime and unexpected. It was back in 1987, at the inaugural Rugby World Cup, that this ability was first witnessed on a global stage. Facing off against joint hosts Australia in the semi-final, the score was tied at 24-24 and the match looked destined to go to extra-time. However, France had other ideas. Starting deep in their own half, Les Bleus ran the ball through the hands of 11 players as they made their way up the pitch. Exceptional offloads and speed allowed them to keep the move alive before a brilliant burst from full-back Serge Blanco saw him score in the corner and win the match.

Right: France full-back Serge Blanco writes his name in the history books by finishing off a brilliant move against Australia.

RUGBY
WORLD CUP™
JAPAN日本2019

THE ROAD TO JAPAN

Less than five months after Richie McCaw lifted the Webb Ellis Cup aloft at Twickenham, qualification for Rugby World Cup 2019 was kicking off. It began in St. Vincent and the Grenadines, where the hosts met Jamaica in the 2016 Rugby Americas North Championship, and ended in November 2018, when for the first time a repechage tournament, between four teams and held over three weekends, decided who claimed the final place at Rugby World Cup 2019.

Right: Canada's players celebrate the team's qualification for Rugby World Cup 2019 after winning the four-team Repechage in November 2018.

HOW THE TEAMS QUALIFIED

The qualification process for Rugby World Cup has grown massively over the years, and for this tournament more than 71 nations fought for a spot in Japan. In all, 188 matches were played, featuring in excess of 3,000 players across six continents. In the end, eight teams booked their place at rugby's biggest event to join the 12 automatic qualifiers from Rugby World Cup 2015.

Just 126 days after Richie McCaw hoisted the Webb Ellis Cup high into the Twickenham sky, the journey to Rugby World Cup 2019 in Japan began, setting out from the unlikely surroundings of Kingstown, St. Vincent.

There, the referee from the final in October, Nigel Owens, officiated the first match of the qualification as St. Vincent and the Grenadines took on Jamaica.

It turned out to be a dream day for the visitors: inspired by their captain and fly-half Hubert Thomas, they won 48-0 in front of a record crowd of 1,000 fans.

It was the perfect start for Rugby World Cup 2019, showcasing how rugby has truly become a global game since the inaugural tournament in 1987.

The 12 teams which had finished in the top three places of their pools at Rugby World Cup 2015 booked automatic berths for the tournament in Japan.

This was a small silver lining for England and Italy, who had missed out on the knockout stages. And for the likes of Japan and Georgia it was a reward for their strong showings in England, and underlined their growth as rugby nations.

The all-encompassing nature of World Rugby means that every full member of the governing body can aspire to play the game at the highest level. As a result, the qualification process led to matches

HOW TEAMS COULD QUALIFY

With 12 places at the tournament in Japan already secured by those teams who finished in the top three of their pools at Rugby World Cup 2015, teams were left to fight for eight places.

THEY WERE DECIDED AS FOLLOWS:
One European qualifier, Europe 1: The highest-ranked team from the Rugby Europe Championships across 2017 and 2018. (Georgia had already qualified by finishing third in their pool at Rugby World Cup 2015). **RUSSIA.**

Two Oceania qualifiers, Oceania 1 and 2: The top two teams from the World Rugby Pacific Nations Cup, played on a home and away basis over June 2016 and 2017. **FIJI** and **TONGA**.

One Europe/Oceania play-off qualifier, Play-off Winner: The third place team from the World Rugby Pacific Nations Cup played a home and away play-off with the second-ranked team in the Rugby Europe Championship (excluding Georgia). The winner on aggregate qualified; the loser was entered into the repechage tournament. **SAMOA**.

Two Americas qualifiers, Americas 1 and 2: Canada and the USA played home and away, the winner on aggregate qualifying. The loser played home and away against the top-ranked South American team (excluding Argentina), and the winner on aggregate qualified for Rugby World Cup 2019. The loser qualified for the repechage tournament. **USA** and **URUGUAY**.

One African qualifier, Africa 1: The winner of the Rugby Africa Gold Cup 2018 qualified for RWC 2019. The runner-up entered the repechage tournament. **NAMIBIA**.

Asia/Oceania play-off for repechage place: The highest-ranked team from the Asia Rugby Championship (excluding Japan) played home and away against the winner of the Oceania Cup. The winner on aggregate (Hong Kong) qualified for the repechage tournament. .

One repechage qualifier: The repechage tournament featured four teams (Canada, Germany, Hong Kong and Kenya) playing in a round-robin format, the winners qualifying. **CANADA**.

taking place all over the world, from Thailand to Mexico.

The USA was the first country to snap up one of the eight qualifying places at the tournament in Japan as they beat Canada over two legs. The first match in Hamilton, Ontario, was a classic encounter between the cross-border rivals and ended in a 28-28 draw.

So there was everything to play for as the two sides met in sunny San Diego on 1 July, 2017, to see who could book a place in Pool C. And it was the Eagles who soared past Canada with a brilliant 52-16 win that included eight tries.

"Today is what we wanted from the start, it's what we've been working for," said USA forward Cam Dolan. "It's the first time we've ever qualified as Americas 1, so to do it on home turf in front of a great crowd is amazing."

Above: The USA was the first country to book their place, beating Canada on aggregate.
Below: Uruguay will be competing in their fourth Rugby World Cup.

Above: Samoa qualified for Rugby World Cup 2019 by beating Germany over two legs, 66-15 in Apia and 42-28 in Heidelberg.

July 2017 proved to be a big month in the qualification process for Rugby World Cup 2019 as first Fiji and then Tonga joined the USA in booking a place at the tournament.

The Oceania spots were to be decided by teams' performances in the World Rugby Pacific Nations Cup across 2016 and 2017, with two sides earning a ticket to Japan.

Fiji earned top spot with a match to spare as they defeated Tonga 14-10 in Nuku'alofa. The reward for the two-time quarter-finalists was a place in Pool D alongside Australia, Wales and Georgia.

"This is a talented group and we have some younger talent emerging also," said Fiji fly-half Ben Volavola. "I believe this squad can improve further and our aim will be to make the quarter-finals in 2019."

A week later, Tonga were celebrating qualification thanks to Fiji's victory over Samoa.

Samoa had needed to get something out of their match with Fiji if they were to secure a spot at Rugby World Cup 2019 and, leading 16-14 at half-time, they were beginning to dream. However, a brilliant fightback from Fiji secured a 38-16 win that left Tonga fans jubilant.

With just five places at Japan 2019 remaining, the pressure was growing, and Canada had another chance to book their spot with a play-off encounter against Uruguay. After losing to the USA, they were determined to grab their second chance. The first leg in Vancouver was a typically tight affair as Uruguay claimed a 38-29 win, meaning it was all to play for in Montevideo. That encounter proved to be even closer: the hosts secured a win, and a place at Rugby World Cup 2019, by just one point, 32-31.

Uruguay's triumph came in February 2018 and a month later it looked as though Romania were joining them after finishing as the highest-ranked team, other than Georgia, in the past two seasons of the Rugby Europe Championship. However, an independent committee three months later revealed that Romania had fielded one ineligible player on eight occasions during

REPECHAGE TABLE

Team	W	D	L	PF	PA	BP	Pts
Canada	3	0	0	121	39	2	14
Germany	2	0	1	79	44	1	9
Hong Kong	1	0	2	61	70	1	5
Kenya	0	0	3	42	150	0	0

the 2017 and 2018 Rugby Europe Championships.

Points deductions and fines followed, meaning Russia took their place in Pool A alongside Ireland, Scotland and Japan.

The same investigation also discovered that Spain had fielded one or more ineligible players on nine occasions during the 2017 and 2018 Rugby Europe Championships. I ike Romania, they were hit with a fine and points deduction, meaning Germany took their place in a European play-off with Portugal.

Germany sneaked through, 16-13, to set up a two-legged encounter with Samoa, in June 2018 but that proved to be a step too far and they lost 108-43 on aggregate.

For Samoa, who feared their Rugby World Cup dream was over when they lost to Fiji in 2017, a place at Japan 2019 was now secured and they joined Pool A.

Just a month later, the seventh spot at the tournament was decided when Namibia sealed the Rugby Africa Gold Cup 2018 title with a 53-28 victory over Kenya.

That meant they edged out Kenya for a place in Pool B in Japan, alongside defending champions New Zealand, South Africa and Italy.

Following Namibia's win there was just one remaining spot to be taken at Rugby World Cup 2019 and in a new format the last place was decided via a repechage tournament in November 2018. Canada, Germany, Hong Kong and Kenya were the four teams battling it out for the last spot, with the quartet playing each other across three weekends in Marseille.

In the end it was Canada who ran out worthy winners as they won all three of their matches to top the round-robin tournament, becoming the 20th and final team to book their ticket to Japan with just under a year to go.

Above: Namibia were unbeaten during the Rugby Africa Gold Cup to secure their place in Japan.

WORLD RUGBY RANKINGS

New Zealand have continued their dominance since the last Rugby World Cup and by the end of 2018 they had kept their place at the top of the rankings. Plenty of sides are vying to knock them off top spot, though, and Japan is the perfect stage for a new side to become number one.

It was all the way back on 16 November, 2009 that New Zealand went to the top of the World Rugby Rankings. South Africa's 20-13 loss to fifth-ranked France in Toulouse cost them 1.72 rating points and their spot as the number one team in the world.

Since then, New Zealand have not surrendered their position at the top of the World Rugby Rankings, and by the end of 2018 they had reigned supreme for nine years. In that time they have won two Rugby World Cups and spent over 3,000 consecutive days as the number one team in the world – a feat that may well never be beaten.

However, there is a sense that the tide could be turning in 2019, with several teams all fighting to knock the All Blacks off top spot. In December 2014, ahead of Rugby World Cup 2015, they had a cushion of over five points between them and second. In December 2018, it was just 1.37.

It was Ireland who were breathing down New Zealand's necks after a stunning 2018 in which they beat the All Blacks for the first time on Irish soil. However, after a stellar 2019 Six Nations, Wales have now emerged as serious contenders to become the number one team in the world.

HOW THEY WORK

The World Rugby Rankings, introduced in 2003, is a system used to rank the world's international teams based on their results, with all countries given a rating between 0 and 100.

The rankings are calculated using a Points Exchange system, in which sides take points off each other based on the match result. Whatever one side gains, the other loses.

The exchanges are based on the match result, the relative strength of each team and the margin of victory, and there is also an allowance for home advantage.

Points exchanges are doubled during Rugby World Cup to recognise the unique importance of the tournament.

Above: New Zealand players perform their traditional pre-match ceremonial challenge: *The Haka*.

Above: Some notable results have kept Fiji riding high in the top 10 of the rankings.

Position, team, points

1	NEW ZEALAND	92.54
2	WALES	89.96
3	IRELAND	88.69
4	ENGLAND	86.27
5	SOUTH AFRICA	84.58
6	AUSTRALIA	82.40
7	SCOTLAND	80.17
8	FRANCE	79.42
9	FIJI	77.95
10	ARGENTINA	77.05
11	JAPAN	75.24
12	GEORGIA	74.42
13	TONGA	73.02
14	ITALY	72.04
15	USA	71.71
16	URUGUAY	69.09
17	SAMOA	68.78
18	ROMANIA	65.84
19	SPAIN	65.11
20	RUSSIA	63.72
21	CANADA	61.36
22	NAMIBIA	60.34
23	PORTUGAL	59.79
24	BRAZIL	58.42
25	HONG KONG	58.11
26	NETHERLANDS	57.60
27	BELGIUM	57.35
28	GERMANY	55.79
29	CHILE	54.04
30	KOREA	53.59
31	KENYA	52.79
32	SWITZERLAND	52.67
33	LITHUANIA	51.53
34	POLAND	50.59
35	UKRAINE	50.25
36	COLOMBIA	49.84
37	PARAGUAY	49.59
38	MALTA	49.48
39	ZIMBABWE	49.28
40	CZECHIA	49.05
41	TUNISIA	48.53
42	UGANDA	48.34
43	SRI LANKA	48.27
44	IVORY COAST	47.55
45	SWEDEN	46.44
46	MOROCCO	46.33
47	MALAYSIA	46.26
48	CAYMAN ISLANDS	45.94
49	CROATIA	45.86
50	MEXICO	45.66

Warren Gatland's side swept all before them to win the Grand Slam, reminding everyone why they will be one of the teams to watch in Japan.

Wales' fine form led to them climbing to second in the world as Ireland dropped to third. In November 2018, Joe Schmidt's side could have gone to the top of the pile after they beat the USA. However, New Zealand's win over Italy ensured they kept their number one status, and now Ireland are playing catch up once again.

Outside of the top three, the chasing pack is still as strong as ever. England cemented their position as the fourth-best team in the world after the 2019 Six Nations, in which they claimed an impressive scalp over Ireland in Dublin as they finished second overall.

Away from the race to catch New Zealand, there is plenty of competition in the World Rugby Rankings. Fiji finished 2018 in good spirits as they soared to an all-time high of eighth courtesy of a first-ever win against France. That pushed Les Bleus down into ninth, but they managed to leapfrog their Pacific Island rivals back into eighth in early 2019 thanks to Six Nations wins over Italy and Scotland.

Outside of the top 10, Georgia continue to be the biggest climbers, and after winning the Rugby Europe Championship in 2019 they moved to 12th in the rankings. Their dream of breaking into the top 10 is slowly becoming a reality.

When the draw for Rugby World Cup 2019 was made, Pool C, featuring Argentina, England and France, was considered 'the Pool of Death'. However, Fiji and Wales' rise in the rankings meant that by March 2019, Pool D had taken on the mantle. Containing three of the top nine teams in the world, with Australia completing the trio, it promises to be a close-fought contest.

MEET THE TEAMS

Reigning champions New Zealand will be looking to win their third Rugby World Cup in a row as the very best from the northern and southern hemispheres go head to head in Japan. In total, 20 nations will battle it out to lift the Webb Ellis Cup and it promises to be a tournament full of drama and memorable moments. Every team will be desperate to go all the way but, as ever, there can be only one winner.

Right: The first nation to successfully defend the trophy, New Zealand will be looking to claim a third Rugby World Cup in a row in Japan in 2019.

All team statistics correct at 18 March, 2019
All player statistics correct at 18 March, 2019

IRELAND

Having reached the quarter-final stage six times but never gone any further, Ireland, at the very least, are expected to break their semi-final duck in Japan. Coached by the innovative and meticulous Joe Schmidt, they have a squad mixed with experience and talent. Now is the time for them to deliver.

RWC STATS

Played:	35
Won	21
Lost:	14
Drawn:	0
Winning percentage:	60%
Points for:	973
Points against:	662
Biggest victory:	64-7 v
	Namibia in Sydney
	on 19 October, 2003
Heaviest defeat:	36-12 v
	France in Durban
	on 10 June, 1995
World Rugby Ranking:	3

COACH

JOE SCHMIDT

In 2013, after winning two European Cups with Irish province Leinster, Joe Schmidt was duly handed the reins of the Ireland national side. The New Zealander has carried his success at club level onto the international stage and is now regarded as one of the best coaches on the planet, particularly after guiding Ireland to only their third ever Six Nations Grand Slam in 2018. A former school teacher, he is strict in ensuring his players uphold his high standards.

Above: Ireland players walk off disconsolately after losing to Wales at Rugby World Cup 2011.

When it comes to Ireland and their history at Rugby World Cup, there is a nagging feeling of what could have been. From the outside looking in, six quarter-final appearances in eight tournaments is a good showing for a country with around 190,000 registered players across all ages and levels.

However, it is the talent produced by the island nation that creates a belief of there definitely being more to come from them. A semi-final berth, or even further, does not seem beyond the bounds of possibility if things go according to plan.

That was certainly the feeling ahead of Rugby World Cup 2015. Led by coach Joe Schmidt they went into the tournament as Six Nations champions, having retained their title from the previous year.

After winning all four matches and topping their pool, Ireland faced Argentina in the quarter-finals. Finally, it looked as

STAR PLAYER

CONOR MURRAY

Position:	Scrum-half
Born:	20 April, 1989, Limerick, Ireland
Club:	Munster (IRE)
Height:	1.88m (6ft 2in)
Weight:	93kg (14st 9lb)
Caps:	72 (+5 Lions)
Points:	85 (14t, 3c, 3p)

Tall, quick, strong and blessed with a brilliant kicking game, Conor Murray is, without a doubt, one of the best scrum-halves in the world. His combination and link-up play with fly-half Johnny Sexton is pivotal to making Ireland tick and they will have a large say in how successful the team is in Japan. Murray was a key part of the British and Irish Lions team who drew the series with New Zealand in 2017, his try in the second test making him the first northern hemisphere player ever to score four career tries against them. A Six Nations Grand Slam winner in 2018, he will be dreaming of more glory in Japan.

IRFU

SCOTLAND

Russia

though a spot in the final four would be secured, but they were blown away by a rampaging Pumas side. In the end, the margin of defeat was more than 20 points. There was much soul-searching done, but things were quickly turned around.

It had been a similar story four years earlier in New Zealand, when Ireland also finished first in their pool after winning all their matches. This time, though, it was Wales who caught Declan Kidney's side off guard with a 22-10 victory.

Other than 2007, when they went out in the pool stages, and 1999, when they were eliminated in the quarter-final play-offs, the last eight has always been Ireland's stumbling block.

It had been the case at the inaugural tournament in 1987 and four years later in 1991 when Australia beat them on both occasions. In 1995 and 2003 France ended their

last-four aspirations, while Wales in 2011 and Argentina, four years later, did likewise.

However, ahead of Rugby World Cup 2019, Ireland are as optimistic as they have ever been.

Schmidt, who has been at the helm since 2013, has turned them into a well-oiled machine that is capable of beating anyone on their day.

Their 40-29 victory over New Zealand in Chicago in November 2016 was a landmark moment as they recorded their first-ever win over the All Blacks at the 29th attempt. It proved Ireland could compete with

the best teams in the world and was just reward for the work Schmidt and his staff have been putting in.

Since then they have kept improving and a Six Nations Grand Slam in 2018 highlighted perfectly the mix of youth and experience available to Schmidt.

They finished off a stellar 2018 by defeating New Zealand 16-9 in Dublin, the first time they have done so on Irish soil. It sparked wild celebrations and a frank admission from New Zealand head coach Steve Hansen, as he declared: "As of now, they are the number one team in the world."

RUGBY WORLD CUP PERFORMANCES

1987	Quarter-final	2003	Quarter-final
1991	Quarter-final	2007	Pool stage
1995	Quarter-final	2011	Quarter-final
1999	Quarter-final play-off	2015	Quarter-final

SCOTLAND

A regular in the knockout stages of Rugby World Cup, Scotland have a rich history in the game. They narrowly missed out on the semi-finals at the last tournament in England, but the attacking brand of rugby promoted by head coach Gregor Townsend is beginning to flourish and expectations are now high in the camp.

Above: Scotland will be aiming to reach their first semi-final since Rugby World Cup 1991.

If it were not for New Zealand, Scotland's Rugby World Cup history might read very differently. For while they have made the knockout stage of every tournament except 2011, it has often been the case that the All Blacks have stood in their way and stopped them from progressing further than the quarter-finals.

That was certainly the situation at the inaugural Rugby World Cup in 1987: after an opening draw with France, Scotland progressed to the quarter-finals courtesy of victories over Zimbabwe and Romania. Waiting for them there were co-hosts New Zealand, who swept them aside with a 30-3 defeat that ended their Rugby World Cup hopes.

Four years later, Scotland achieved their best performance to date by reaching the semi-finals as they played hosts alongside England, France, Ireland and Wales. Home advantage, however, was not enough to get them

RWC STATS

Played:	38
Won	22
Lost:	15
Drawn:	1
Winning percentage:	57.89%
Points for:	1,142
Points against:	748
Biggest victory:	89-0 v

Ivory Coast in Rustenburg on 26 May, 1995

Heaviest defeat:	51-9 v

France in Sydney on 25 October, 2003

World Rugby Ranking:	7

COACH

GREGOR TOWNSEND
Appointed as Scotland head coach in May 2017, Gregor Townsend has carried on the fine work of his predecessor Vern Cotter. Under Cotter, Scotland made the quarter-finals of Rugby World Cup 2015 and Townsend will have similar aspirations in Japan. The former fly-half has implemented an attacking style of rugby, just as he did during his five years in charge of Glasgow Warriors, with whom he won the PRO12 title in 2015.

IRFU

SCOTLAND

Russia

STAR PLAYER

FINN RUSSELL

Position: .... Fly-half
Born: .... 23 September, 1992,
Bridge of Allan, Scotland
Club: .... Racing 92 (FRA)
Height: 1.83m (6ft)
Weight: 91kg (14st 4lb)
Caps: 44
Points: 135 (5t, 31c, 16p)

When it comes to creativity and flair, there are few fly-halves in the world who can match Finn Russell. Always willing to try the unexpected, he has the ability to unlock defences with a single pass. It was under current Scotland head coach Gregor Townsend that Russell made his professional debut for Glasgow Warriors and he is now flourishing with him at international level too. The fly-half, who can also operate at centre, has since moved to France for his club game, and that has only aided his development. A risk-taker who loves to play close to the gain-line, Russell will be one to watch in Japan.

over the line as England edged past them 9-6 at Murrayfield to book a place in the final. New Zealand subsequently beat Scotland in the third-place play-off.

In 1995 and 1999, the All Blacks again stood in Scotland's way, defeating them in the quarter-finals on both occasions. It meant that in three of the first four Rugby World Cups, Scotland had been knocked out by New Zealand.

Scotland continued their run of quarter-final exits at Rugby World Cup 2003 after finishing second in Pool B behind France. That earned them a showdown with hosts Australia, who defeated them 33-16 on their way to the final. Four years later in France, they were sent home at the same stage: this time it was Argentina, the surprise package, who overcame them with a narrow 19-13 victory.

Scotland's record of reaching the knockout stage of every Rugby World Cup ended in 2011, when for the first time they were eliminated in the pool stage. Defeats to England and Argentina led to them finishing third in Pool B, but the pain of that exit has proved to be a catalyst going forward.

Head coach Vern Cotter guided them to the quarter-finals of Rugby World Cup 2015, where they were defeated 35-34 by Australia after fly-half Bernard Foley kicked a last-minute penalty.

Cotter's successor, Gregor Townsend took charge in 2017 and has since carried on his good work. The new head coach masterminded a first win over in England in a decade during the 2018 Six Nations and there is a belief that Scotland can upset the odds in Japan.

Townsend has imposed an attacking and creative style of rugby, and Scotland will expect to get out of their pool, which contains Ireland, Japan, Russia and Samoa.

That would set up a quarter-final match with either the winner or runner-up of Pool B – which includes, you guessed it, New Zealand.

RUGBY WORLD CUP PERFORMANCES

1987	Quarter-final	2003	Quarter-final
1991	Semi-final	2007	Quarter-final
1995	Quarter-final	2011	Pool stage
1999	Quarter-final	2015	Quarter-final

JAPAN

After defeating two-time world champions South Africa at the last tournament, Japan head into Rugby World Cup 2019 full of optimism. The hosts have continued to grow under head coach Jamie Joseph, who has carried on the work of his predecessor Eddie Jones, and they are dreaming of a first-ever quarter-final appearance.

RWC STATS

Played:	28
Won:	4
Lost:	22
Drawn:	2
Winning percentage:	14.29%
Points for:	526
Points against:	1,259
Biggest victory:	52-8 v Zimbabwe in Belfast on 14 October, 1991
Heaviest defeat:	145-17 v New Zealand in Bloemfontein on 4 June, 1995
World Rugby Ranking:	11

COACH

JAMIE JOSEPH

After guiding the Highlanders to the Super Rugby title in 2015, Jamie Joseph made the move into international coaching by taking charge of Japan in 2016. The former flanker, who played for Japan and New Zealand during his playing career, had big shoes to fill by following on from Eddie Jones. However, he has developed Japan into a dangerous attacking team by refreshing the squad with players who did not feature at Rugby World Cup 2015.

Above: Karne Hesketh scores the winning try against South Africa at Rugby World Cup 2015.

When Eddie Jones revealed, ahead of Rugby World Cup 2015, that Japan were aiming to reach the quarter-finals, more than a few eyebrows were raised. Jones had developed Japan immensely during his time as head coach, which included a run of 10 straight wins from 2013-14 and a World Rugby Ranking high of ninth, but the idea of a march to the knockout stage seemed a step too far.

However, the Australian's ambition suddenly appeared realistic after their opening match of the tournament, when Japan stunned two-time world champions South Africa. It was a match that undeniably goes down as one of the greatest in rugby history, so much so that a film commemorating it is in production.

Wing Karne Hesketh was the hero that day in Brighton, as his last-

STAR PLAYER

KENKI FUKUOKA

Position:	Wing
Born:	7 September, 1992, Fukuoka, Japan
Club:	Sunwolves (JPN)
Height:	1.75m (5ft 9in)
Weight:	83kg (183lb)
Caps:	29
Points:	90 (18t)

A member of Japan's squad from Rugby World Cup 2015, Kenki Fukuoka has developed into one of the most exciting wings on the planet. Blessed with electric pace and a brilliant side-step, he already boasts an impressive try record despite having years ahead of him. Fukuoka will undoubtedly be one of the quickest players at the tournament in Japan, but he is also deceptively strong too. Since taking charge Japan head coach Jamie Joseph has encouraged his players to be expressive and get the ball out wide; a style of play that has suited Fukuoka perfectly. He could be one of the stars of the tournament.

minute try secured a 34-32 victory that left everyone in shock. Forgotten in the aftermath of the match was that Japan could have kicked a penalty to force a draw, but they elected to go for the win and kicked for touch to set up the drama.

"Today is just the start. The target now is to make the quarter-finals and we have got Scotland in four days' time, so we cannot rest on our laurels," said Jones, who is coaching England at this Rugby World Cup.

Ultimately Japan fell just short of their target, despite gaining two more wins, over Samoa and the USA. They finished with three wins, more than they had managed in their previous seven tournaments combined, but Scotland progressed ahead of them in second place from Pool B by virtue of having more bonus points.

Nevertheless, Japan's victory over South Africa has changed the rugby landscape in the country. "If you are a child in Japan, you will watch this and you will want to play rugby for Japan in the next World Cup," Jones asserted.

The Australian was right: interest in the game has boomed since 2015 and the fact that Japan are hosts has only added to the buzz. Prior to their memorable journey at Rugby World Cup 2015, Japan had endured a difficult time at the tournament since its creation in 1987. Other than 1991, they failed to win a single match.

The success of 2015 feels like a watershed moment, though, and new head coach Jamie Joseph has helped push them forward.

Crucially they are beginning to show they can compete with Six Nations and Rugby Championship teams, as demonstrated by their 34-17 victory over Italy in June 2018. In the November of that year they also managed to score five tries against New Zealand during a 69-31 loss, while they led England 15-10 at half-time at Twickenham before losing 35-15.

Full of creativity and energy, Japan will be out to shock the world again – this time as hosts. And, after 2015, no one should write them off.

RUGBY WORLD CUP PERFORMANCES

1987	Pool stage	2003	Pool stage
1991	Pool stage	2007	Pool stage
1995	Pool stage	2011	Pool stage
1999	Pool stage	2015	Pool stage

RUSSIA

Russia are competing in only their second ever Rugby World Cup after qualifying for the 2019 edition of the tournament. Their debut appearance was in 2011, but they failed to record a victory in New Zealand. The Russians' aim in Japan in 2019 is to secure that elusive first-ever competition victory.

RWC STATS

Played:	4
Won	0
Lost:	4
Drawn:	0
Winning percentage:	0%
Points for:	57
Points against:	196
Biggest victory:	N/A
Heaviest defeat:	62-12 v Ireland in Rotorua on 25 September, 2011
World Rugby Ranking:	20

COACH

LYN JONES

Handed the reins in August 2018, Lyn Jones has had little time to prepare Russia for Rugby World Cup 2019. Not that the former Wales flanker is complaining: this is the first time he has been given the chance to coach at an international level. Previously Jones has enjoyed stints with club sides Ospreys, London Welsh and Newport Gwent Dragons, and before Russia came calling he had coached in Namibia with Welwitschias, the national squad development team.

Above: Russia are back for their second Rugby World Cup after missing out in 2015.

After being appointed head coach of Russia just over a year out from Rugby World Cup 2019, Lyn Jones pulled no punches when describing the task ahead of him.

"My appointment was going to be for the long term, but since then we've been handed an opportunity to play in the World Cup, which gives me a bit of an Everest in front of me," Jones told BBC Sport Wales.

"We're excited, the players are delighted and it's going to be the most exciting year of their rugby career. They're focused, and Russian boys work hard, they're disciplined and they're proud."

In the months before Jones' appointment, it transpired that Russia had won a place at Rugby World Cup 2019, when they feared qualification had passed them by. Investigations by World Rugby discovered that Belgium, Romania and Spain

STAR PLAYER

VASILY ARTEMYEV

Position:	Full-back/wing
Born:	24 July, 1987, Moscow, Russia
Club:	Krasny Yar Krasnoyarsk (RUS)
Height:	1.83m (6ft)
Weight:	87kg (13 st 10lb)
Caps:	84
Points:	153 (30t, 1p)

Vasily Artemyev is arguably Russia's most high-profile player and he is no stranger to fans of the English Premiership. Able to operate at full-back or on the wing, he spent two seasons in England with the Northampton Saints from 2011-13. That came off the back of Artemyev's impressive performances in New Zealand at Rugby World Cup 2011, where he scored a try against Ireland – the country where he spent seven years studying at college and university during his younger years. He goes into this tournament with plenty of experience and he is expected to captain the team in Japan.

had all fielded ineligible players during the qualification competition. The trio were subsequently hit with points deductions and Romania's place went to Russia instead.

Having been given a second chance to compete in Japan, Jones and Russia are determined to grab the opportunity with both hands. Prior to this tournament, the country have competed in only one other Rugby World Cup.

That came back in 2011, when they qualified for rugby's showpiece event by finishing second in the 2008–10 European Nations Cup behind winners Georgia. After securing a spot in New Zealand, Russia acquitted themselves well during their debut appearance. They narrowly lost their opening match 13-6 to the USA, earning themselves their first-ever Rugby World Cup bonus point. Three defeats to the established nations of Australia,

Ireland and Italy followed, but there will still be plenty of positives to take forward.

Now the challenge for Jones is to try and secure a first-ever Rugby World Cup win for Russia as they prepare to face off against Ireland, Scotland, Japan and Samoa in Pool A. It will be no easy task for Russia, who failed to qualify for the last tournament.

However, if Rugby World Cup 2015 taught us anything, it is that no country can be ruled out when it comes to crunch time.

"We saw huge performances from Japan and Namibia in the last World

Cup, so anything can happen on the day," said Jones. "There's a lot of good rugby players in Russia, and it's a sleeping giant."

Whether Russia can awaken in Japan remains to be seen, but they do have the ability to cause problems. Full-back Vasily Artemyev has experience of playing in the English Premiership due to a spell with Northampton Saints, while second-row Andrei Ostrikov has been with Sale Sharks since 2011. Fly-half Yuri Kushnarev is the country's all-time leading points scorer and is deadly from the kicking tee.

RUGBY WORLD CUP PERFORMANCES

1987	Did not enter		2003	Did not qualify
1991	Did not enter		2007	Did not qualify
1995	Did not qualify		2011	Pool stage
1999	Did not qualify		2015	Did not qualify

SAMOA

Western Samoa burst onto the scene in 1991, when they reached the quarter-finals of Rugby World Cup during their debut appearance. They repeated that feat four years later, but since then Samoa have struggled to go deep at the tournament despite causing opposing sides plenty of headaches.

Above: Western Samoa stunned the rugby world when they beat Wales, in Cardiff, in 1991.

RWC STATS

Played:	28
Won	12
Lost:	16
Drawn:	0
Winning percentage:	42.86%
Points for:	654
Points against:	732
Biggest victory:	60-13 v
	Uruguay in Perth
	on 15 October, 2003
Heaviest defeat:	60-10 v
	South Africa in Brisbane
	on 1 November, 2003
World Rugby Ranking:	17

COACH

STEVE JACKSON

Appointed as the head coach of Samoa in September 2018, Steve Jackson was one of 40 candidates to apply for the job. The New Zealander landed the role after impressing as the head coach of North Harbour and as an assistant at Super Rugby side the Blues. Despite having little time to implement his style with Samoa, Jackson has big ambitions for his side in Japan and is targeting a place in the quarter-finals.

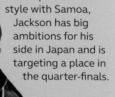

Western Samoa did not enter the inaugural Rugby World Cup in 1987, and little was expected of them four years later as they prepared to make their debut. Indeed ahead of the tournament, which was co-hosted by England, France, Ireland, Scotland and Wales, they were regularly described as "minnows". People were soon eating their words.

Drawn in Pool 3 alongside Argentina, Australia and Wales, Western Samoa were expected to make up the numbers. However, they stunned Wales in their opening match by defeating the hosts 16-13 in front of a crowd of 45,000 at Cardiff Arms Park.

It was a monumental result and one that stunned the rugby community, who were now beginning to realise how the game was expanding all across the world.

For the Western Samoans, it was a

STAR PLAYER

CHRIS VUI

Position:	Second row
Born:	11 February, 1993, Auckland, New Zealand
Club:	Bristol Bears (ENG)
Height:	2.00m (6ft 6in)
Weight:	118kg (18st 8lb)
Caps:	12
Points:	5 (1t)

Having made his debut for Samoa in 2016, Chris Vui was made captain of the team within a year – making him the youngest skipper of all the top 20 sides in the world. Despite his age, the second row, who can operate in the back row too, has emerged as a leader within the team and he is a key part of their plans. Vui is well known to fans in England after enjoying a stint with the Worcester Warriors, and then joining the Bristol Bears in 2017. An athletic forward who is dangerous in the loose and an excellent jumper at lineouts, the New Zealand-born Vui will certainly be one to watch in Japan.

memorable day too. One, indeed, that they would never forget, summed up by the fact that try-scorer To'o Vaega went on to name his son Cardiff in honour of the win.

A narrow 9-3 defeat to Australia was followed up by a 35-12 win over Argentina and a place in the quarter-finals. Scotland proved to be too strong for them there, winning 28-6 at Murrayfield, but Western Samoa was now well and truly on the rugby map.

Four years later, they again proved their credentials by making the quarter-finals after finishing second to England in a pool containing Argentina and Italy. This time it was eventual winners South Africa who sent them home, but once more they had demonstrated how they could compete against the biggest rugby nations.

By 1999 Western Samoa had become Samoa and any idea of them being minnows was well and

truly gone. Instead they were known as one of the most physical sides in the tournament – a quality they still possess today.

They made it out of their pool again at Rugby World Cup 1999, losing in a quarter-final play off to Scotland, but since then their record has stuttered.

Samoa have not been in another knockout match since then, having been eliminated in the pool stages of the last four tournaments. Admittedly the draw has not been kind to them. In both 2003 and 2007, they were in the same pool as England and South Africa.

However, there will have been no hiding their disappointment at the last Rugby World Cup where they won just once and lost to Japan.

Samoa's form since then has been mixed and they finished bottom of the combined table for the Pacific Nations Cup for 2016 and 2017, meaning that they had to overcome Germany in a play-off to qualify for Japan.

Defeats in November 2018 to Georgia and the USA have added to concerns, but the fact remains that Samoa still have the pace, power and desire to cause any team problems on their day.

RUGBY WORLD CUP PERFORMANCES

1987	Did not enter	2003	Pool stage
1991	Quarter-final	2007	Pool stage
1995	Quarter-final	2011	Pool stage
1999	Quarter-final play-off	2015	Pool stage

RUGBY UNITES A NATION

24 June, 1995: Ellis Park, Johannesburg

If anyone is trying to learn about the power of the game, they need look no further than Rugby World Cup 1995. Following the abolition of apartheid, South Africa had been readmitted to the international set-up and were duly made hosts of the tournament. After beating Australia in their first match, a wave of emotion swept the country and the Springboks never looked back. They went on to beat New Zealand 15-12 in the final thanks to Joel Stransky's drop goal in extra-time. Nelson Mandela, dressed in a Springbok jersey, subsequently presented South Africa captain Francois Pienaar with the Webb Ellis Cup in a moment that has gone down in history. A nation was united and rugby had been at the heart of it.

Right: President Nelson Mandela presents South Africa captain Francois Pienaar with the Webb Ellis Cup after they defeated New Zealand in the final of Rugby World Cup 1995 in Johannesburg.

NEW ZEALAND

The reigning champions are looking to make history at Rugby World Cup 2019 as they bid to become the first country to lift the Webb Ellis Cup three times in a row. The All Blacks have remained the dominant team in the world since the last tournament and will be the favourites in Japan.

RWC STATS

Played:	50
Won:	44
Lost:	6
Drawn:	0
Winning percentage:	88%
Points for:	2,302
Points against:	681
Biggest victory:	145-17 v Japan in Bloemfontein on 4 June, 1995
Heaviest defeat:	22-10 v Australia in Sydney on 15 November, 2003
World Rugby Ranking:	1

COACH

STEVE HANSEN

Assistant to Graham Henry at Rugby World Cup 2011, Steve Hansen was made head coach after that tournament, where the All Blacks had gone all the way. He has picked up where his predecessor left off, ensuring New Zealand retained the Webb Ellis Cup four years later in England. Since then, Hansen has guided the All Blacks to three Rugby Championship titles in a row, and also drew a series against the British and Irish Lions in 2017.

Above: New Zealand became the first team to win back-to-back Rugby World Cups in 2015.

It may seem difficult to comprehend, but there was a time when the All Blacks' air of invincibility at Rugby World Cup was not as strong as it is today.

They won the inaugural tournament as co-hosts back in 1987, and some were expecting New Zealand to dominate for years to come. With outstanding performances from the likes of John Kirwan and Grant Fox, they had swept all before them to be the first team to lift the Webb Ellis Cup.

Indeed, in the final against France, they won by 20 points.

Four years later, at an expanded Rugby World Cup, New Zealand were knocked out in the semi-finals by an Australia team who would go on to lift the trophy.

At Rugby World Cup 1995, the All Blacks were still hurting and desperate to regain their crown. With the unstoppable Jonah Lomu in their ranks, they

STAR PLAYER

KIERAN READ

Position:	Number eight
Born:	26 October, 1985, Papakura, New Zealand
Club:	Crusaders (NZL)
Height:	1.93m (6ft 4in))
Weight:	111kg (17st 7lb)
Caps:	118
Points:	125 (25t)

Replacing the legendary Richie McCaw as captain of the All Blacks was never going to be an easy task, but Kieran Read has more than stepped up to the plate. Appointed as skipper in 2016 following McCaw's retirement after Rugby World Cup 2015, Read has led from the front. A phenomenal athlete with brilliant handling skills and vision, he is a threat in both attack and defence. Named World Rugby Player of the Year in 2013, he has more than 100 caps to his name, and a third Rugby World Cup triumph in Japan would cement his place as an All Black legend.

scored an incredible 222 points in the pool stages. Come the final, however, it was South Africa celebrating, defeating them 15-12 after extra-time.

Semi-final exits followed in the next two tournaments. Suddenly, the triumph of 1987 was beginning to feel a long way away.

The biggest low, though, was still to come: in 2007, for the first time, New Zealand failed to make it to the semi-finals. The pool stages had been a breeze as they scored 309 points, but they were stunned in the quarter-finals by hosts France.

Initially, the All Blacks led 13-3 and looked set for a spot in the final four, but a stunning comeback from Les Bleus left them shell-shocked.

If anything was going to spark New Zealand back into life, it was hosting Rugby World Cup 2011. By then, 24 years had passed since they had been world champions and a nation was

waiting expectantly for the glory days to return to the Land of the Long White Cloud.

Led by Richie McCaw, they duly delivered, battling an injury crisis that forced out three fly-halves Their fourth, Stephen Donald – a replacement for Aaron Cruden in the final – kicked the decisive penalty as the All Blacks saw off France in a tight final, 8-7. He had started the tournament on a fishing holiday; he left it a world champion.

Since then, the dominant All Blacks we know have roared back. Four years later, in England, they

conquered all before them once again, to become the first team to retain the Webb Ellis Cup. They ran in three tries to see off Australia 34-17 at Twickenham.

Three Rugby Championships in a row followed in the wake of that triumph and coach Steve Hansen will be keen for more success in Japan.

New Zealand will rightly head into the tournament as favourites – and they will take some stopping. However, anything can happen at a Rugby World Cup, and the other countries will be out to end the All Blacks' era of dominance.

RUGBY WORLD CUP PERFORMANCES

1987	WORLD CHAMPIONS	2003	Semi-final
1991	Semi-final	2007	Quarter-final
1995	Runners-up	2011	WORLD CHAMPIONS
1999	Semi-final	2015	WORLD CHAMPIONS

SOUTH AFRICA

POOL B

Although prevented from entering the first two Rugby World Cups, South Africa have lifted the Webb Ellis Cup twice. Renowned as one of the most competitive and physical sides on the planet, the Springboks are always contenders to go all the way at any Rugby World Cup. Japan will be no different.

RWC STATS

Played:	36
Won:	30
Lost:	6
Drawn:	0
Winning percentage:	83.33%
Points for:	1,250
Points against:	486
Biggest victory:	87-0 v

Namibia in Auckland on 22 September, 2011

Heaviest defeat:	29-9 v

New Zealand in Melbourne on 8 November, 2003

World Rugby Ranking:	5

COACH

RASSIE ERASMUS
Following the departure of Allister Coetzee, Rassie Erasmus was named the new head coach of South Africa in March 2018, despite originally joining in a broader role as director of rugby. He made a bright start to his tenure, defeating England in a three-test June series and finishing second in the 2018 Rugby Championship – South Africa's best performance since 2014. Erasmus will now be hoping for more success in Japan as he prepares to coach at his first Rugby World Cup.

Above: Damian de Allende is among a clutch of Springboks hoping to peak in 2019.

After South Africa lost the first match of their Rugby World Cup campaign four years ago to Japan, it looked as though they could be on an early flight home. However, in a manner that sums up their attitude, they fought back and finished third at the tournament.

Such a result maintained South Africa's impressive record at Rugby World Cups. To date, they have competed in six of the eight tournaments, going all the way twice. Two quarter-final appearances and two trips to the semi-finals complete the set.

It was back in 1995 that South Africa first got their hands on the Webb Ellis Cup. They had missed the first two tournaments through a sporting exile that had been enforced due to the apartheid regime in their country.

The end of apartheid also brought an end to their absence from rugby's greatest show and they marked their arrival in

STAR PLAYER

EBEN ETZEBETH

Position:	Second row
Born:	29 October, 1991, Cape Town, South Africa
Club:	Stormers (RSA)
Height:	2.04m (6ft 8in)
Weight:	123kg (19st 5lb)
Caps:	75
Points:	15 (3t)

When it comes to imposing and powerful second rows, there are few who fit the bill as well as Eben Etzebeth. Standing more than two metres tall, the forward is often described as "a monster" and since making his South Africa debut in 2012 he has lived up to his early promise. The Springboks have a proud history of producing world-class second rows, such as Victor Matfield, and Etzebeth looks destined to go down in the history books as another great. Incredibly effective in the lineout and the loose, he will have a big impact on how far South Africa go in Japan.

memorable fashion. Carried forward on a wave of emotion, South Africa went all the way on home soil as the power of rugby was demonstrated. The game had united a nation – as demonstrated by Nelson Mandela dressing in a Springbok jersey to present South Africa captain Francois Pienaar with the Webb Ellis Cup.

Four years later in Wales, South Africa's quest for glory was halted in the semi-finals as Australia knocked them out in extra-time. In 2003 the Springboks were sent home earlier, this time by a rampant New Zealand in the quarter-finals.

However, by 2007, South Africa had developed a side with a formidable pack, perfectly supported by the deadly goal-kicking of full-back Percy Montgomery. They duly went all the way in France, defeating England 15-6 in the final. They have yet to taste

such success again: their semi-final finish in 2015 had been preceded by a quarter-final exit in New Zealand four years earlier.

There is a growing hope among those in South Africa that they could upset the odds in Japan. After a disappointing time under Allister Coetzee, who was sacked in February 2018, the Springboks have begun to show signs of promise under new head coach Rassie Erasmus.

The strength of the team historically has been in the forwards and, in Eben Etzebeth and Lood de Jager, they have

one of the best second row pairings in the world. Behind them, Faf de Klerk has become one of the most dangerous scrum-halves, while fly-half Handré Pollard has lived up to his billing since making his debut in 2014.

Out wide, Aphiwe Dyantyi has made a bright start to his international career replacing the retired wing Bryan Habana, and full-back Willie le Roux has rediscovered his best form.

It all makes for a potent South Africa team and one that, as history has shown us, cannot be overlooked when it comes to the crunch.

RUGBY WORLD CUP PERFORMANCES

1987	Did not enter	2003	Quarter-final
1991	Did not enter	2007	WORLD CHAMPIONS
1995	WORLD CHAMPIONS	2011	Quarter-final
1999	Semi-final	2015	Semi-final

ITALY

POOL B

Italy have appeared at every Rugby World Cup since the tournament's inception in 1987. However, they have so far failed to make it past the pool stages. Now coached by Irishman Conor O'Shea, Italy will be hoping they can upset the odds in Japan and book a first quarter-final appearance.

RWC STATS

Played:	28
Won:	11
Lost:	17
Drawn:	0
Winning percentage:	39.29%
Points for:	529
Points against:	899
Biggest victory:	53-17 v Russia in Nelson on 20 September, 2011
Heaviest defeat:	101-3 v New Zealand in Huddersfield on 14 October, 1999
World Rugby Ranking:	14

COACH

CONOR O'SHEA

After six successful years as Harlequins' Director of Rugby, Conor O'Shea made the jump to international coaching with Italy in 2016. The Irishman has embraced the role since becoming head coach as he looks to develop the game at all levels. O'Shea is determined to build Italy into a strong rugby nation that will prosper even when he has left his post. He guided Italy to their first-ever win over South Africa in November 2016.

Above: Italy are aiming to make the knockout stages of a Rugby World Cup for the first time.

In a country where football is the main sport, it is sometimes overlooked just how much rugby is growing in Italy. Ever since they competed in the inaugural Rugby World Cup, the game has been developing year after year.

The first tournament in New Zealand and Australia nearly yielded what Italy have always craved – a quarter-final place. Drawn in a pool with New Zealand, Argentina and Fiji, Italy earned one win, the same as Argentina and Fiji, though it was the latter who progressed to the knockout stages by virtue of scoring more tries.

The next three Rugby World Cups proved to be a learning curve for Italy, who achieved just two wins. The 1999 edition was a particularly painful experience, when for the first time the Azzurri failed to win a pool match.

From that disappointment came a drive to push forward. Italy joined the Six Nations Championship in 2000, and

ALL BLACKS

SPRINGBOKS

ITALIA

NAMIBIA RUGBY
RUGBY

STAR PLAYER

JAKE POLLEDRI

Position:	Back row
Born:	8 November, 1995, Bristol, England
Club:	Gloucester (ENG)
Height:	1.89m (6ft 2in)
Weight:	106kg (234lb)
Caps:	8
Points:	5 (1t)

Born in Bristol, Jake Polledri qualifies to play for Italy by virtue of his Italian grandparents. The back-row forward is relatively new to the squad, making his debut in 2018, but he has quickly become a key part of head coach Conor O'Shea's plans. A powerful ball-carrier, Polledri has had to fight hard to make his way in the game. Rejected by Bristol in his youth, he was offered a place at Hartpury College before Gloucester snapped him up. Since then he has gone from strength to strength and there are some who question how England let Polledri slip through their net. England's loss is Italy's gain.

earned their first win in their opening match, defeating Scotland 34-20. By playing against the best sides in the northern hemisphere, Italy continued to develop as a rugby nation, and they defeated Wales during the 2003 Six Nations.

More positives came at that year's Rugby World Cup, when for the first time they won two matches at the same tournament. Four years later in France they achieved the same feat and narrowly missed out on a spot in the quarter-finals by losing their crunch pool match with Scotland 18-16. The 2011 and 2015 editions of the tournament told the same tale too as again Italy recorded two victories each time, finishing third in their pool on both occasions.

The aim now is to finally make that big step and reach the quarter-finals of a Rugby World Cup. Under new head coach Conor O'Shea, there have been signs of promise, with their first-ever win over South Africa in November 2016 a particular highlight. A defeat to Japan in June 2018 caused some concern, but a victory over Georgia calmed some nerves heading into 2019.

The truth is, O'Shea is thinking much more long-term than the Rugby World Cup in Japan. The Irishman is working to create pathways for players in Italy to ensure that the country has a side who can compete with the very best in the future.

As O'Shea has pointed out already, things are not going to change overnight, but green shoots from his work are beginning to show.

"Molto a fare, molto a fatto," O'Shea told the BBC shortly after he got the Italy job in 2016. He translated it as, "So much done and so much to do," and added, "but it's exciting."

With South Africa and defending champions New Zealand standing in their way in Pool B, the Italians are going to have to be at their very best to improve on the team's previous-best third place finish in their pool.

RUGBY WORLD CUP PERFORMANCES

1987	Pool stage	2003	Pool stage
1991	Pool stage	2007	Pool stage
1995	Pool stage	2011	Pool stage
1999	Pool stage	2015	Pool stage

NAMIBIA

After making their Rugby World Cup debut in 1999, Namibia are still on the hunt for a first-ever win at the tournament as they head to Japan. They have steadily improved over the years and their exposure to the world's top sides has helped the game develop in the country.

RWC STATS

Played:	19
Won	0
Lost:	19
Drawn:	0
Winning percentage:	0%
Points for:	214
Points against:	1,148
Biggest victory:	N/A
Heaviest defeat:	142-0 v Australia in Adelaide on 25 October, 2003
World Rugby Ranking:	22

Above: Namibia made their Rugby World Cup debut in 1999 and they continue to progress.

COACH

PHIL DAVIES
Appointed as Namibia's head coach just three months before Rugby World Cup 2015, Phil Davies had little time to prepare his team for that tournament. However, the former Wales forward is now four years into the job and his hard work is beginning to pay off. Under Davies, Namibia won all five of their matches in the Rugby Africa Gold Cup 2018, which secured their place in Japan. Now he is targeting a first Rugby World Cup victory.

So far, Rugby World Cup has provided Namibia with some very painful memories. Since qualifying for their first-ever tournament in 1999, they have played 19 matches without registering a victory. To make matters worse, 11 of those defeats have seen the opposition score 50 points.

It makes for painful reading, but it is easy to forget that this is a country which only gained independence in 1990 – three years after the first Rugby World Cup in New Zealand and Australia.

Just nine years after Namibia had gained independence, they were competing in the tournament and were taught some harsh lessons on their debut. Fiji and France both recorded victories over them while Canada, who they will face again this year, also defeated them 72-11.

Four years later, they

STAR PLAYER

CLIVEN LOUBSER

Position:	Fly-half
Born:	24 February, 1997, Rehoboth, Namibia
Club:	UP Tuks (RSA)
Height:	1.76m (5ft 9in)
Weight:	75kg (11st 11lb)
Caps:	13
Points:	144 (4t, 47c, 10p)

Cliven Loubser was just two years old when Namibia made their Rugby World Cup debut in 1999, but now the young fly-half will be hoping he can guide his team to their first-ever win at the tournament. Since making his test debut in June 2017 against Russia, Loubser has showed composure and experience beyond his years. He has quickly become a key player for Namibia and a man for the big occasion, as shown by his 22-point haul against Kenya in the decisive match of the Rugby Africa Gold Cup 2018. Japan could be the perfect stage for him to shine and maybe the first of many Rugby World Cups.

suffered a 142-0 loss to hosts Australia in what was the lowest point of their history. On that occasion, poor tackling allowed the Wallabies to run riot, but since then things have changed.

By the time Rugby World Cup 2007 came around, a young Jacques Burger had emerged on the scene. The flanker, who is now retired, installed a new mentality of dogged defence and at that tournament they lost to Ireland by a more respectable 32-17.

While the 2011 edition may have been a tall order after being drawn in the "Pool of Death" with South Africa, Wales, Samoa and Fiji, Rugby World Cup 2015 proved to be Namibia's most competitive showing so far.

They lost 58-14 to New Zealand, but a first try against the All Blacks sparked wild celebrations on the bench. Namibia went on to push Tonga all the way in a 35-21 defeat,

while they earned a first-ever Rugby World Cup point by losing 17-16 to Georgia.

The country's improved performance in England four years ago came under head coach Phil Davies, who had been given the job just three months before the tournament started. The Welshman has since had more time to implement his ideas and there is optimism that a first Rugby World Cup win could be on the cards.

Legendary flanker Burger may have gone, but in Cliven Loubser the Welwitschias have an exciting fly-half

driving them forward. The squad has plenty of experience too from players such as centre Darryl de la Harpe, who captained the side during their autumn tour in 2018.

Drawn alongside New Zealand, South Africa, Italy and Canada, Namibia will be targeting the Canucks as they try to claim a first Rugby World Cup win.

Twenty years ago at their first tournament, the Welwitschias met Canada and were defeated by a margin of 61 points. Japan will be a true marker of how far Namibia have come since then.

RUGBY WORLD CUP PERFORMANCES

1987	Did not enter	2003	Pool stage
1991	Did not enter	2007	Pool stage
1995	Did not qualify	2011	Pool stage
1999	Pool stage	2015	Pool stage

CANADA

Canada boasts a proud Rugby World Cup history after appearing in every tournament since its inception back in 1987. The Canucks reached the quarter-finals in 1991, but in more recent times they have struggled to match those heights. After four defeats at Rugby World Cup 2015, they are determined to produce a better showing in Japan.

RWC STATS

Played:................................29
Won....................................7
Lost:..................................20
Drawn:.................................2
Winning percentage:..........24.14%
Points for:..........................527
Points against:......................838
Biggest victory:................72-11 v
Namibia in Toulouse
on 14 October, 1999
Heaviest defeat:...............79-15 v
New Zealand in Wellington
on 2 October, 2011
World Rugby Ranking:...............21

COACH

KINGSLEY JONES
Following the departure of Mark Anscombe, Canada turned to Kingsley Jones in September 2017 to guide them to Rugby World Cup 2019. The Welshman duly delivered just over a year later, when he ensured the Canucks won the final place in Japan by defeating Kenya, Germany and Hong Kong in the repechage tournament. The triumph was the latest achievement for Jones to add to his CV, which already includes spells with the Dragons and Sale Sharks, as well as Russia.

Above: Canada are still trying to repeat their 1991 success when they were quarter-finalists.

The Rugby World Cup has witnessed some of rugby's biggest teams come unstuck against apparently lesser opposition. Take Wales losing to Western Samoa in 1991 or, in the last tournament in England, when Japan stunned the two-time world champions South Africa by scoring a try in the last minute to beat them.

Such memorable moments show how rugby has grown over the years to encompass teams from all over the world. In truth, Canada were one of the first teams to prove that there are no underdogs at a Rugby World Cup.

Indeed, in the inaugural tournament in 1987 the Canucks won their opening match 37-4 against Tonga. Defeats against Ireland and Wales followed, but four years later it was a different story.

That time around, at Rugby World Cup 1991, Canada made it out of their pool in second

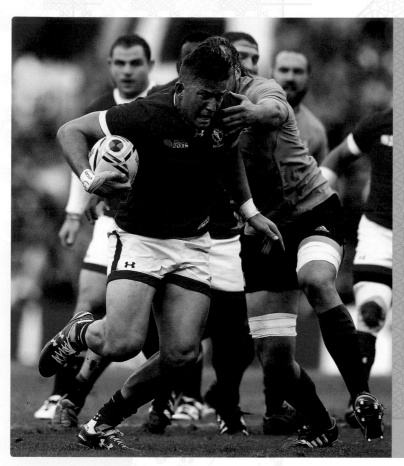

STAR PLAYER

DTH VAN DER MERWE

Position:	Wing
Born:	28 April, 1986, Worcester, South Africa
Club:	Glasgow Warriors (SCO)
Height:	1.83m (6ft)
Weight:	98kg (15st 6lb)
Caps:	55
Points:	185 (37t)

Born in South Africa, Daniel Tailliferre Hauman van der Merwe and his family emigrated to Canada in 2003. The wing, who can also operate at centre, pledged his allegiance to the Canucks and he has gone on to become the top try scorer in the country's history. Van der Merwe boasts a particularly impressive record at Rugby World Cups, scoring tries in all four of Canada's pool matches in England four years ago. Japan will be his fourth tournament and it would not be wise to bet against him adding to his tally of six tries in 12 Rugby World Cup matches.

place behind France after victories over Fiji and Romania. A place in the quarter-finals was their reward and they nearly pulled off another shock there, going down 29-13 to defending champions New Zealand.

Just like Western Samoa, who stunned Wales in that tournament to reach the quarter-finals too, Canada had demonstrated that no one could be written off at a Rugby World Cup. The precedent had been set and upsets have continued ever since.

For Canada, however, their star began to fade after their memorable showing at the 1991 tournament. Ahead of the next one in South Africa, they had defeated the likes of France and Wales, but in the pool stages they were drawn alongside Australia and South Africa and knocked out.

The 1999 and 2003 editions of the tournament proved difficult too

because Canada recorded just two wins. The disappointment was even greater in France, at Rugby World Cup 2007, when for the first time in their history they failed to record a single victory.

The Canucks improved their standing four years later in New Zealand by claiming a win and a draw, but a winless performance in England at Rugby World Cup 2015 has them fired up for Japan.

Their road to Rugby World Cup 2019 has not been easy and in truth they would have hoped to qualify some 18 months before they did.

Defeats to the USA and Uruguay forced them to earn qualification through the first-ever repechage tournament.

This took place over three weekends in Marseille, in November 2018, and Canada recorded comprehensive victories over Kenya, Germany and Hong Kong to finish at the top of the group and claim the coveted final berth at the tournament.

It brought an end to what has been a bumpy qualification journey for the Canucks. They will be hoping events in Japan run more smoothly.

RUGBY WORLD CUP PERFORMANCES

1987	Pool stage	2003	Pool stage
1991	Quarter-final	2007	Pool stage
1995	Pool stage	2011	Pool stage
1999	Pool stage	2015	Pool stage

LOMU ANNOUNCES HIMSELF BY HITTING ENGLAND FOR FOUR

18 June, 1995: Newlands Stadium, Cape Town

When Jonah Lomu arrived at Rugby World Cup 1995, little was known about the wing who had just two All Black caps. However, by the time he left South Africa, Lomu was the name on everyone's lips. He was in devastating form during the tournament, in particular against England in the semi-final. Try as they might, the England defence just could not stop the huge wing – whose pace and power was far superior to anyone else's. Lomu went on to score four tries in the match, his first one typifying his dominance. Receiving a loose pass from Graeme Bachop outside the 22, he beat two defenders before running over England full-back Mike Catt. New Zealand went on win 45-29 and a star was born.

Right: Wing Jonah Lomu was an almost unstoppable force at Rugby World Cup 1995, and he finished as the tournament's top try-scorer with seven to his name.

ENGLAND

After the pain of Rugby World Cup 2015, England are hungry for success as they head to Japan. As hosts of the last tournament, they were eliminated in the pool stages, their quest for glory ending after just three matches. Now coached by Eddie Jones, they have rebuilt and are on the hunt for glory.

England Rugby

RWC STATS

Played:	44
Won:	31
Lost:	13
Drawn:	0
Winning percentage:	70.45%
Points for:	1,379
Points against:	708
Biggest victory:	111-13 v
	Uruguay in Brisbane
	on 2 November, 2003
Heaviest defeat:	36-0 v
	South Africa in Saint-Denis
	on 14 September, 2007
World Rugby Ranking:	4

COACH

EDDIE JONES

Appointed as England head coach in November 2015, Eddie Jones arrived in the role with a wealth of experience. He was in charge of Australia when they lost to England in the final of Rugby World Cup 2003, and was an assistant helping to take South Africa all the way four years later. After stints with Saracens and Suntory Sungoliath, Jones masterminded Japan to three wins at Rugby World Cup 2015 – including an historic victory over South Africa.

Above: In 2003 England were the first northern hemisphere team to win the Rugby World Cup.

Rugby World Cup 2015 may have been a success in terms of the smooth running of the tournament itself, but for England as a team it was a moment of heartache.

The hosts went into their own competition dreaming of success in front of an expectant fan base.

However, after an opening day victory over Fiji, back-to-back defeats against Wales and Australia meant that England were out after three matches. A victory over Uruguay offered scant consolation as it was the first time that a host nation had gone out in the pool stages of a Rugby World Cup.

Such anguish seemed a lifetime away from the joy of 2003, when England were crowned champions of the world for the first time.

Prior to that, England's success at Rugby World Cups had been a case of "so near, but yet so far". In 1987, at the inaugural tournament in New

STAR PLAYER

MARO ITOJE

Position:	Second row
Born:	28 October, 1994, London, England
Club:	Saracens (ENG)
Height:	1.98m (6ft 5ins)
Weight:	115kg (18st 2lbs)
Caps:	27 (+3 Lions)
Points:	5 (1t)

When Maro Itoje made his England debut in February 2016, head coach Eddie Jones vowed he would turn the then 21-year-old "from a Vauxhall Viva into a BMW". True to his word, the second row has developed into one of the most powerful forwards in the game. After breaking into the England team, Itoje capped off 2016 by being named European Player of the Year thanks to his role in helping Saracens win the Champions Cup. Superb in the lineout and dynamic in the loose, Itoje has become a regular for England and was also part of the British and Irish Lions tour to New Zealand in 2017.

Zealand and Australia, they were eliminated at the quarter-final stage by Wales. Four years later, this time on home soil, they made it all the way to the final – only for Australia to defeat them 12-6.

A semi-final exit in South Africa at Rugby World Cup 1995 was followed by another quarter-final finish four years later.

That one came under the stewardship of coach Clive Woodward, who believed something special was brewing despite the disappointment of crashing out 44-21 to South Africa.

Woodward was to be proved right: over the next four years, England developed into a formidable team. By the time they headed to Australia for Rugby World Cup 2003, they had already beaten the Wallabies in their own backyard – as well as the mighty All Blacks.

Led by captain Martin Johnson, Woodward's men went all the way Down Under as a dramatic drop goal from Jonny Wilkinson won the final 20-17 against Australia with seconds to spare in extra-time.

There were hopes that this would be the start of an era of dominance for England, but it was not to be.

A spirited effort brought them to the final again four years later, but South Africa, who had defeated them in their opening pool match, proved too strong again.

A third quarter-final exit occurred in New Zealand, where the team, now coached by Johnson, were knocked out 19-12 by France.

Since Eddie Jones replaced Stuart Lancaster after Rugby World Cup 2015, green shoots of optimism have emerged. He led England to the Six Nations Grand Slam in 2016, when his side went the whole calendar year unbeaten, including a 3-0 series win in Australia.

England retained their Six Nations title the following year and now, after a dip in form in 2018, Jones and England will have their eyes on making a mark in Japan at Rugby World Cup 2019.

RUGBY WORLD CUP PERFORMANCES

1987	Quarter-final		2003	WORLD CHAMPIONS
1991	Runners-up		2007	Runners-up
1995	Semi-final		2011	Quarter-final
1999	Quarter-final		2015	Pool stage

FRANCE

Despite appearing in three Rugby World Cup finals, France are still yet to lift the Webb Ellis Cup. Les Bleus were runners-up at the inaugural tournament back in 1987 and they have continued to be a threat since then. Blessed with some of the finest athletes in world rugby, they can beat any side on their day.

RWC STATS

Played:	48
Won	33
Lost:	14
Drawn:	1
Winning percentage:	68.75%
Points for:	1,487
Points against:	895
Biggest victory:	87-10 v
	Namibia in Toulouse
	on 16 September, 2007
Heaviest defeat:	62-13 v
	New Zealand in Cardiff
	on 17 October, 2015
World Rugby Ranking:	8

COACH

JACQUES BRUNEL

Handed the reins in December 2017 following the dismissal of Guy Novès, Jacques Brunel is no stranger to international rugby. He was forwards coach for France from 2001-07, working under the now Fédération Française de Rugby President Bernard Laporte. Brunel helped turn the French pack into a formidable unit as they won the Six Nations Grand Slam in 2002 and 2004. He enjoyed success at club level with Perpignan before coaching Italy at the last Rugby World Cup.

Above: France can always pull off an upset, as shown by their win over New Zealand in 2007.

When it comes to France's Rugby World Cup story, there is a strong feeling of what might have been. Three times they have made it to the final of rugby's showpiece event and three times they have walked away as runners-up.

France are capable of beating anyone and they have produced some of the tournament's most memorable moments over the years. Capable of the sublime and the unbelievable, it would be foolish to write off Les Bleus.

A glimpse of what was to come from France was shown at the very first Rugby World Cup in 1987. There, in New Zealand and Australia, they marched to the final after a brilliant performance in the semi-final. They had looked to be heading out when taking on Australia, but a moment of magic from full-back Serge Blanco in the dying stages set up a showdown with New Zealand. By then,

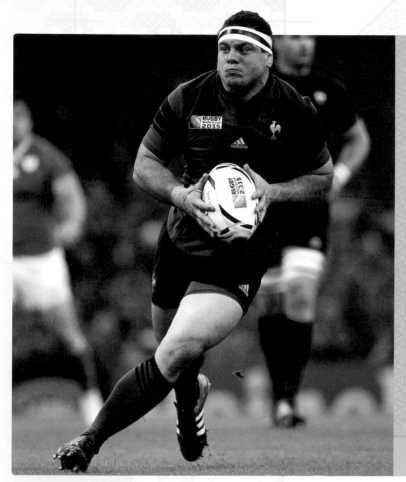

STAR PLAYER

GUILHEM GUIRADO

Position:	Hooker
Born:	17 June, 1986, Ceret, France
Club:	Toulon (FRA)
Height:	1.83m (6ft)
Weight:	105kg (16st 7lb)
Caps:	68
Points:	40 (8t)

Born in Ceret in the south of France, Guilhem Guirado began his professional career with Perpignan. The hooker was part of a golden age for the club and he helped them become Top 14 champions in 2009. Guirado's form at club level naturally led to him gaining international recognition and he made his debut for France in March 2008, off the bench against Italy. Lauded for his exceptional work ethic and discipline, the front row forward soon became a starter and he played four of Les Bleus' matches at Rugby World Cup 2015, scoring one try in the process. He was appointed captain after the tournament.

though, they had run out of steam and France were defeated 29-9.

After a disappointing quarter-final exit at the tournament in 1991, when France were co-hosts, Les Bleus proceeded to go on a run of making at least the semi-finals at the next six Rugby World Cups.

In 1995 they were narrowly defeated by eventual winners South Africa in the semi-final, while four years later they were in the final again. This time it was Australia who defeated them, running out 35-12 winners in Cardiff.

Two more trips to the semi-final duly followed as again French fans were treated to the agony of being so close, yet so far, to their goal of seeing their country lift the Webb Ellis Cup. By the time Rugby World Cup 2011 rolled into town, France were being written off – despite their proud history. Again, they defied

the critics and odds, reaching the final and losing by a single point to hosts New Zealand. Once more, Les Bleus' dreams of becoming world champions had been crushed at the final hurdle.

France may have lost to New Zealand by a solitary point in the final in 2011, but they were convincingly beaten by them four years later in England at the quarter-final stage. The All Blacks ran out 62-13 winners in Cardiff – the scene of Les Bleus' magical victory in 2007 – and, for the first time since 1991, France failed to make it to the semi-finals.

France will be determined to return there in Japan, but they find themselves in one of the toughest pools at the tournament. They are drawn alongside Argentina and England, so booking a place in the quarter-finals could prove a challenge, especially as their recent Six Nations form has not been at the level their fans expect of them.

Les Bleus will know, though, that if they perform to their best they can beat anyone on their day. They have shown as much in the past, and the hope will be that Japan is finally their moment in the sun.

RUGBY WORLD CUP PERFORMANCES

1987	Runners-up	2003	Semi-final
1991	Quarter-final	2007	Semi-final
1995	Semi-final	2011	Runners-up
1999	Runners-up	2015	Quarter-final

ARGENTINA

Argentina's performances at Rugby World Cups have improved dramatically since they made their debut at the first tournament back in 1987. They truly marked their arrival at the game's top table in 2007, when they finished third. Another run to the semi-finals in England four years ago only underlined how much they have improved.

Above: Argentina came of age at Rugby World Cup 2007 when they won the bronze final.

RWC STATS

Played:	37
Won	19
Lost:	18
Drawn:	0
Winning percentage:	51.35%
Points for:	992
Points against:	748
Biggest victory:	67-14 v
Namibia in Gosford on 14 October, 2003	
Heaviest defeat:	46-15 v
New Zealand in Wellington on 1 June, 1987	
World Rugby Ranking:	10

COACH

MARIO LEDESMA

After making over 80 appearances for Argentina as a player, Mario Ledesma is now leading Los Pumas into a Rugby World Cup as their head coach. Given the job after Daniel Hourcade resigned in June 2018, Ledesma has had to work quickly to get his ideas across. This is the former hooker's first spell as head coach of an international team, having previously been in charge of the Jaguares in Super Rugby and forwards coach for Australia.

In many ways, Argentina are the shining example for any aspiring rugby nation. More than three decades ago, at the first Rugby World Cup, Los Pumas were one of the smallest sides at the tournament. Some viewed them as a team simply making up the numbers while the likes of Australia, England and New Zealand battled it out for the Webb Ellis Cup.

Finishing bottom of their pool did little to dispel that idea, but now Argentina are a different story. They can boast two trips to the semi-finals as part of their Rugby World Cup CV, while they now also compete in the Rugby Championship alongside Australia, New Zealand and South Africa. So much for being there to make up the numbers.

However, it has by no means been easy for Argentina to climb their way up the rugby ladder. After a disappointing performance at Rugby World Cup 1987, they

STAR PLAYER

AGUSTÍN CREEVY

Position:	Hooker
Born:	15 March, 1985, La Plata, Argentina
Club:	Jaguares (ARG)
Height:	1.81m (5ft 11in)
Weight:	110kg (243lb)
Caps:	83
Points:	15 (3t)

Agustín Creevy may no longer be Argentina captain, but he remains a key part of head coach Mario Ledesma's set-up. Creevy has established himself as one of the best hookers in the world during his career and his experience will be vital to Los Pumas as they bid for glory in Japan. Accurate and efficient at the set-piece, the forward is so dynamic in the loose that he has been capped by Argentina at flanker before. The most-capped Argentina captain in history, he is now helping new skipper Pablo Matera settle into the role.

went out at the pool stages of the next two tournaments.

They were, though, showing signs of improvement and a trip to the quarter-finals in 1999 showed a glimpse of what was to come. They defeated Ireland 28-24 in the quarter-final play-offs to reach the last eight and, while they may have been knocked out by France, the seeds had been sown for future success. The fact that fly-half Gonzalo Quesada finished as the tournament's top points scorer merely underlined the country's strong showing.

A dip in performance led to an exit in 2003 at the pool stage, but four years later in France Los Pumas announced their arrival on the big stage. An opening match win over the hosts paved the way for a magical run to the semi-finals, where they were beaten by eventual winners South Africa.

Argentina have been riding the crest of a wave since then and have established themselves among rugby's top teams. After they reached the quarter-finals of Rugby World Cup 2011, they joined the Rugby Championship. The yearly competition means they continually test themselves against Australia, New Zealand and South Africa and it has only aided their development.

In England four years ago, Argentina provided one of the stories of the tournament in their quarter-final victory over Ireland. It was not just the win, it was the manner it was

achieved, running in four tries in a 43-20 victory. Their supporters will be hoping that Argentina can deliver on the biggest stage once again, but repeating that semi-final feat may prove tricky, not least because they have been drawn alongside England and France.

Los Pumas will fancy their chances at causing their opponents plenty of problems, however, as recent history has shown that Rugby World Cup seems to bring out the best in them. England and France certainly should not expect to have things all their own way.

RUGBY WORLD CUP PERFORMANCES

1987	Pool stage	2003	Pool stage
1991	Pool stage	2007	Semi-final
1995	Pool stage	2011	Quarter-final
1999	Quarter-final	2015	Semi-final

USA

USA RUGBY

The USA are regular participants at Rugby World Cups, appearing in every tournament bar the 1995 edition. So far, they have failed to shine on the biggest stage, their total number of wins standing at three. However, under new head coach Gary Gold, they will be out to cause an upset in Japan.

RWC STATS

Played:	25
Won	3
Lost:	22
Drawn:	0
Winning percentage:	12%
Points for:	350
Points against:	892
Biggest victory:	39-26 v Japan in Gosford on 27 October, 2003
Heaviest defeat:	64-0 v South Africa in London on 7 October, 2015
World Rugby Ranking:	15

COACH

GARY GOLD

Having been appointed as the USA's new head coach in January 2018, Gary Gold has made a strong start. He led them to a perfect record in the Americas Rugby Championship early that year before defeating Scotland in June – the first time the Eagles had ever beaten a major rugby nation. Gold has a wealth of experience in the game after spells with clubs sides such as Bath and the Sharks, as well as South Africa.

Above: USA wing Takudzwa Ngwenya skips past South Africa star Bryan Habana to score.

It seems increasingly likely that one day the USA will become a major rugby power. The sport is rapidly growing in popularity and it is beginning to attract the attention of aspiring athletes who are hungry for success on the world stage. Given the size and financial backing available to the USA, one would think it is only a matter of time before they make the knockout stages of the Rugby World Cup. A finish better than fourth in Pool C in 2019 would be seen as a step in the right direction.

However, for now, the Eagles' record at the Rugby World Cup indicates they are still developing as a rugby nation. Despite qualifying for all but the 1995 tournament, they have managed to win only three matches.

The first of those came in their very first match, back at the inaugural tournament in 1987. There they defeated this

STAR PLAYER

BLAINE SCULLY

Position: Full-back/Wing
Born: 29 February, 1988, Sacramento, USA
Club: Cardiff Blues (WAL)
Height: 1.91m (6ft 3in)
Weight: 93kg (14st 9lb)
Caps: 46
Points: 60 (12t)

There are few players who have contributed more to the growth of rugby in the USA than Blaine Scully. The full-back, who can easily operate on the wing too, has forged a professional career in Europe with spells at Leicester Tigers and Cardiff Blues – and he has paved the way, with Chris Wyles, for others to follow suit. Scully has been a driver of the game back in the USA too and he is the co-founder of United States Rugby Players' Association. Now heading into his third Rugby World Cup, Scully will lead the Eagles after being appointed captain in 2016.

year's hosts Japan 21-18 in a close encounter.

The USA had to wait till 2003 to claim their next victory: the tournaments in between proved barren affairs. Their time in Australia, though, turned out to be one of their best performances, offering evidence of how the game was beginning to grow back home.

The Eagles narrowly lost their opening match 19-18 to Fiji, before beating Japan 39-26. Their final fixtures against France and Scotland ended in defeat, but on both occasions they gave good accounts of themselves.

Since then there have been flashes of brilliance, such as wing Takudzwa Ngwenya's try against South Africa at Rugby World Cup 2007, when he managed to skip past none other than the legendary Bryan Habana to score. However, other than victory

over Russia at the 2011 tournament, there has been little else for Eagles fans to cheer about.

That could well change in Japan, though, as the USA are heading to Asia after one of their best qualifying campaigns ever. Previously, they have been late to the party, but victory over Canada in July 2017 has given them two years to prepare.

The growth of the game has also been aided by the advent of Major League Rugby, which has provided players in Canada and the USA with a professional competition to compete in. Naturally that has caused the

player pool to swell and the benefits are already being seen.

In June 2018, the USA claimed their first win over a major rugby nation as they defeated Scotland 30-29 in Houston. Every member of the 23-man squad selected by head coach Gary Gold that day was being paid to play their rugby – which was not always the case in the past.

The USA Sevens team have made it to the top table. Now all Eagles fans will be hoping their 15-a-side squad can enjoy success in Japan, against their pool rivals Argentina, England, France and Tonga.

RUGBY WORLD CUP PERFORMANCES

1987	Pool stage	2003	Pool stage
1991	Pool stage	2007	Pool stage
1995	Did not qualify	2011	Pool stage
1999	Pool stage	2015	Pool stage

TONGA

One of the most competitive and physical teams at Rugby World Cup 2019, Tonga will be out to upset the odds in Japan. Unlike their Pacific Island neighbours, Fiji and Samoa, they have never made the knockout stages. However, they have shown that on their day they can beat any team.

RWC STATS

Played: 25
Won 7
Lost: 18
Drawn: 0
Winning percentage: 28%
Points for: 405
Points against: 861
Biggest victory: .... 29-11 v
**Ivory Coast in Rustenburg
on 3 June, 1995**
Heaviest defeat: .... 101-10 v
**England at Twickenham
on 15 October, 1999**
World Rugby Ranking: 13

COACH

TOUTAI KEFU
After earning 60 caps for Australia during his playing career, Toutai Kefu is now coaching the country of his birth, Tonga. The former number eight has previously worked as assistant and interim coach, but he was given the head coach job full-time in 2016. Prior to that, Kefu spent four years in charge of Japanese club side Kubota Spears. A Rugby World Cup winner as a player in 1999, this is his debut tournament as a coach.

Above: Tonga will be looking to emulate their success in 2011, when they upset France 19-14.

When it comes to natural talent and physical prowess, there are few sides in the world who can match Tonga. The Pacific island has produced some of the game's most imposing and powerful players over the years, including flanker Nili Latu and number eight Finau Maka, among a number of others.

The likes of Maka and his predecessors enjoyed great success in the club game, and now the Tongan stars of today are hoping for success on the international stage.

There is once again plenty of talent in their squad. Sonatane Takulua offers them zip and energy from scrum-half and he will be tasked with marshalling their powerful pack around as they bid for glory in Japan.

Tonga's early performances at Rugby World Cups proved to be a sharp learning curve. At the inaugural tournament in 1987,

STAR PLAYER

SIALE PIUTAU

Position: .... Centre
Born: .... 13 October, 1985,
Auckland, New Zealand
Club: .... Bristol Bears (ENG)
Height: 1.85m (6ft 1in)
Weight: 98kg (218lb)
Caps: 35
Points: 15 (3t)

Now set to take part in his third Rugby World Cup, Siale Piutau has established himself as a key part of Tonga's side. The centre is expected to captain the team in Japan and he will no doubt lead from the front. A regular for the Bristol Bears in England, it is there that he plays alongside his brother, Charles, who is capped by New Zealand. Tonga will look to Piutau to provide physicality in Japan, but there is more to his game than just brute force. A phenomenal competitor and leader, he will be vital if Tonga are to upset the odds this time around.

they finished bottom of their pool after losing all three of their matches – although a 29-16 loss to Wales did show signs of promise.

After failing to qualify four years later, they returned to the world stage in 1995. There, in South Africa, they recorded their first Rugby World Cup victory over the Ivory Coast. However, the match was overshadowed by an injury to the Ivory Coast's Max Brito, which left him paralysed.

A 28-25 win over Italy at the 1999 edition of the tournament appeared to be a watershed moment, but a disappointing performance at Rugby World Cup 2003 proved otherwise. Tonga lost all four of their pool matches in Australia but their disappointing showing acted as catalyst for change.

By the time the tournament arrived in France, four years

later, they were a different beast altogether, boasting a raft of talented players including Latu and Maka. Tonga duly went on to record two victories at a Rugby World Cup for the first time, beating both Samoa and the USA. Ultimately, it was only a narrow 30-25 loss to champions-in-waiting South Africa that stopped them going through to the quarter-finals.

Tonga carried that momentum into Rugby World Cup 2011, where they enjoyed undoubtedly their finest hour to date by defeating eventual finalists France 19-14. In truth, the

win should have booked Tonga a place in the quarter-finals, but an earlier defeat to Canada meant that Les Bleus sneaked through instead of them via bonus points.

A solitary win at the last tournament, their worst performance since 2003, has made Tonga hungry for success in Japan. It will not be an easy task for them, however: they have been drawn in one of the toughest pools alongside Argentina, England, France and USA.

Whatever happens though, you can be sure that Tonga will give even the toughest of opponents a stern test.

RUGBY WORLD CUP PERFORMANCES

1987	Pool stage		2003	Pool stage
1991	Did not qualify		2007	Pool stage
1995	Pool stage		2011	Pool stage
1999	Pool stage		2015	Pool stage

WILKINSON KICKS ENGLAND TO GLORY

22 November, 2003: Telstra Stadium, Sydney

As pressure kicks go, few can rival that of England fly-half Jonny Wilkinson's winning drop goal against Australia in the final of Rugby World Cup 2003. With less than a minute of extra-time remaining, and the scores tied at 17-17, scrum-half Matt Dawson fired the ball to Wilkinson from the base of a ruck. The fly-half calmly took the ball from outside the 22 and, with a swing of his weaker right foot, stroked the ball between the posts. It left a stunned Australia with just 26 seconds to reply and England duly held on to be crowned champions of the world. Captain Martin Johnson went on to lift the Webb Ellis Cup high into the Australian sky on a night England and Wilkinson would never forget.

Right: Jonny Wilkinson wrote himself into English sporting history by stroking over the winning drop goal against Australia in the final of Rugby World Cup 2003.

POOL D

AUSTRALIA

Having lifted the Webb Ellis Cup on two occasions, Australia have a proud Rugby World Cup record. Crowned world champions for the first time in 1991, they repeated the feat eight years later in Wales. Now they will be hoping to defy the odds and win it for the third time in Japan.

RWC STATS

Played:	48
Won:	39
Lost:	9
Drawn:	0
Winning percentage:	81.25%
Points for:	1,645
Points against:	646
Biggest victory:	142-0 v Namibia in Adelaide on 25 October, 2003
Heaviest defeat:	34-17 v New Zealand at Twickenham on 31 October, 2015
World Rugby Ranking:	6

COACH

MICHAEL CHEIKA
Following the shock resignation of Ewen McKenzie in October 2014, Michael Cheika stepped up to coach the Wallabies with less than a year to go until Rugby World Cup 2015. Australia shone at the tournament, knocking England out in the pool stages and getting all the way to the final before losing to New Zealand. Voted World Rugby Coach of the Year a day later, Cheika will be dreaming of more success in Japan this time.

Above: Australia were dominant in the 1990s as they won the Rugby World Cup twice.

No matter what their form when arriving at a Rugby World Cup, Australia, more than any other nation, have a knack of delivering on the big stage. Something about the opportunity of lifting the Webb Ellis Cup just seems to spur them on and they have an impressive record in the competition.

It was during the 1990s that they enjoyed their greatest period of dominance. The inaugural tournament in 1987 had been a disappointment: though co-hosts, they were eliminated at the semi-final stage by France thanks to a stunning try finished off by Serge Blanco.

However, four years later they were crowned world champions. Their side then was a formidable unit – boasting talents such as David Campese, John Eales and Michael Lynagh. They were worthy winners, defeating England 12-6 in front of a packed and stunned Twickenham.

Rugby World Cup 1995 in South Africa proved to be a disappointing

STAR PLAYER

MICHAEL HOOPER

Position:	Flanker
Born:	29 October, 1991, Sydney, Australia
Club:	Waratahs (AUS)
Height:	1.82m (6ft)
Weight:	101kg (15st 8lb)
Caps:	91
Points:	85 (17t)

Since making his international debut in 2012 against Scotland, Michael Hooper has developed into a key component of Australia's side. Now the team's captain, he leads by example from the front and is undeniably one of the best flankers on the planet. Often finishing matches with the highest turnover count of any player, he is deceptively dangerous in the loose too when attacking. A two-time winner of the John Eales Medal, which is awarded to honour the best Australian player each year, Hooper will be absolutely crucial to the Wallabies' fortunes in Japan.

affair when England got revenge on Australia and knocked them out at the quarter-final stage. However, four years later, the Wallabies were once again in the northern hemisphere lifting the Webb Ellis Cup.

By now the likes of Campese and Lynagh had moved on, but the production line of green and gold talent had not stopped. George Gregan and Stephen Larkham had emerged as two excellent half-backs, while Tim Horan and Joe Roff added to a dangerous backline.

They conquered all before them and were crowned world champions for a second time, with a 35-12 win over France in the final summing up their dominance.

Since then, however, Australia have been waiting to get their hands back on the Webb Ellis Cup. As hosts of Rugby World Cup 2003, they were undone in the final by a last minute

Jonny Wilkinson drop goal in extra-time that led to England being crowned winners.

Four years later, in France, it was England thwarting them again – this time at the quarter-final stage as their scrum proved too strong.

After that painful loss, Australia's record has improved. In 2011 they made it all the way to the semi-finals – only for New Zealand to knock them out, though there was consolation of victory in the bronze final. Four years on they went one step further, to the final – but again the All Blacks were there, waiting for them.

That loss at Rugby World Cup 2015 was tough for the Wallabies to take, but their ability to make the final should not be overlooked. As the tournament began, few predicted them to go far, but they clicked into gear at just the right time.

They have endured more rocky patches since then, including a third-place finish in the 2018 Rugby Championship, and home series losses to both England –3-0 in 2016 – and Ireland – 2-1 in 2018. However, as history has shown us, you can never write off the Wallabies when it comes to crunch time.

RUGBY WORLD CUP PERFORMANCES

1987	Semi-final	2003	Runners-up
1991	WORLD CHAMPIONS	2007	Quarter-final
1995	Quarter-final	2011	Semi-final
1999	WORLD CHAMPIONS	2015	Runners-up

WALES

Wales will be determined to make Rugby World Cup 2019 a memorable affair as their head coach Warren Gatland will be stepping down afterwards. Gatland has been in charge for more than a decade and he led Wales to the semi-finals in 2011. This time, he is determined to go all the way.

RWC STATS

Played:	37
Won:	21
Lost:	16
Drawn:	0
Winning percentage:	56.76%
Points for:	1,049
Points against:	718
Biggest victory:	81-7 v Namibia in Cardiff on 26 September, 2011
Heaviest defeat:	49-6 v New Zealand in Brisbane on 14 June, 1987
World Rugby Ranking:	2

Above: Rugby World Cup 2011 ended in heartbreak for Wales after a semi-final defeat.

COACH

WARREN GATLAND

There are few coaches in world rugby who can boast a CV to match Warren Gatland. Over the years he has won multiple honours at club and international level, while he never lost a series during his two stints in charge of the British and Irish Lions. The head coach of Wales since 2007, Gatland will be stepping down after the tournament. His replacement, Wayne Pivac, has some big shoes to fill.

It is fair to say that until the appointment of Warren Gatland as head coach in November 2007, Wales' performances at Rugby World Cups were mixed. From semi-final finishes to crashing out in the pool stages after shock defeats to the likes of Western Samoa, Wales in the early days gave their supporters a range of highs and lows.

Their performance at the first tournament in 1987 remains their joint-best finish to date. Wales travelled to New Zealand and Australia dreaming of going all the way, and they topped their pool ahead of Ireland. Victory over rivals England set up a semi-final meeting with New Zealand, but they were blown away 49-6 by an All Blacks team which went on to lift the Webb Ellis Cup.

After that strong showing, expectations were

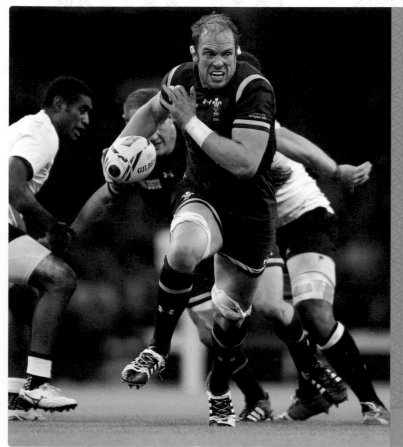

STAR PLAYER

ALUN WYN JONES

Position:	Second row
Born:	19 September, 1985, Swansea, Wales
Club:	Ospreys (WAL)
Height:	1.98m (6ft 6in)
Weight:	118kg (18st 8lb)
Caps:	125 (+9 Lions)
Points:	45 (9t)

Alun Wyn Jones has established himself as one of the best second rows in the world during a glittering playing career. A veteran of three British and Irish Lions tours, he is one of only seven Lions players to have beaten Australia, New Zealand and South Africa. For Wales, Jones has been key too. Superb in the lineout, he is crucial also for his leadership on the pitch and he will captain the side in Japan. This will be Jones' fourth Rugby World Cup and he will be absolutely vital to Wales' aspirations of going deep into the tournament once again.

high as Wales acted as co-hosts for Rugby World Cup 1991. However, it turned out to be a disappointing campaign as Western Samoa defeated them 16-13 in Cardiff. Wales never recovered and went out in the pool stages.

Four years later, it was a similar story: again they failed to get out of their pool. However, this time their exit could at least be explained by being drawn alongside Ireland and New Zealand.

Consecutive quarter-final appearances at the 1999 and 2003 editions of the tournament marked an upturn in form, but a third pool exit in 2007 proved to be decisive. Wales were eliminated after defeat to Fiji, and in November Gatland was installed as head coach.

The New Zealander had an immediate impact, guiding Wales to the Six Nations Grand Slam

the following year. By the time Rugby World Cup 2011 had rolled around, Gatland had created a formidable side that was capable of beating anyone.

They enjoyed a brilliant run to the semi-finals in Gatland's home country, only to be knocked out 9-8 by France in a match that saw captain Sam Warburton sent off after just 19 minutes. It was a cruel end to what had been a fantastic tournament for Wales.

After reaching the quarter-finals at the last Rugby World Cup, Gatland, who was Ireland's coach

at Rugby World Cup 1999, is now targeting the Webb Ellis Cup. He is due to step down at the end of the tournament, with Wayne Pivac ready to replace him, and he is determined to end on a high.

Gatland has every reason to be optimistic, though, as his side had quietly gone about their business prior to securing a third Six Nations Grand Slam of his reign in 2019. That came after Wales won all four of their November 2018 tests for the first time.

Japan could well turn out to be Gatland's perfect swansong.

RUGBY WORLD CUP PERFORMANCES

1987	Semi-final	2003	Quarter-final
1991	Pool stage	2007	Pool stage
1995	Pool stage	2011	Semi-final
1999	Quarter-final	2015	Quarter-final

GEORGIA

Considered the most dominant force in Europe of countries outside of the Six Nations, Georgia have greatly improved after appearing at their first Rugby World Cup back in 2003. Renowned for producing some of the best scrummagers in the world, several of their forwards play their club rugby in France.

RWC STATS

Played:	16
Won	4
Lost:	12
Drawn:	0
Winning percentage:	25%
Points for:	197
Points against:	524
Biggest victory:	30-0 v
	Namibia in Lens
	on 26 September, 2007
Heaviest defeat:	84-6 v
	England in Perth
	on 12 October, 2003
World Rugby Ranking:	12

COACH

MILTON HAIG
Recommended to Georgia by former Scotland coach Vern Cotter and the New Zealand Rugby Union, Milton Haig has impressed since taking charge in 2011. He achieved his target of two wins at Rugby World Cup 2015 – Georgia's best ever performance at a tournament. Having worked with New Zealand's under-20s and the Maori All Blacks, Haig has flourished during his first role as head coach of an international side. He will be targeting more success in Japan.

Above: Georgia will look to make the most of their fearsome power in the scrum.

Looking back at Georgia's Rugby World Cup debut 16 years ago in Australia, it is remarkable to see how far they have come since then. That time around, they opened with an 84-6 defeat to England and finished with a 24-12 loss to Uruguay. In between that, Samoa and South Africa both beat them by scoring 46 points each.

It was a painful start for Georgia, but considering the country had only gained independence in 1991 it was always going to take time for them to find their feet on rugby's biggest stage.

At Rugby World Cup 2007, supporters were treated to a glimpse of what was to come. Georgia recorded their first-ever win at the tournament, a 30-0 victory over Namibia.

More importantly they gave Ireland an almighty scare in Bordeaux. Trailing 10-7 early in the second half, Ireland were forced to fight back, and ended up clinging on to secure a

STAR PLAYER

MIKHEIL NARIASHVILI

Position:	Prop
Born:	25 May, 1990, Kutaisi, Georgia
Club:	Montpellier (FRA)
Height:	1.85m (6ft 1in)
Weight:	118kg (260lb)
Caps:	54
Points:	5 (1t)

In the words of head coach Milton Haig, Georgian players are simply born to scrum. Mikheil Nariashvili certainly is and the prop has established himself as one of the best loose-heads in the world. Renowned for his work in the scrum, Nariashvili has given countless players an afternoon they would rather forget. The prop is also more than useful in the loose and his tackle and carry counts are usually among the highest of his team. If Nariashvili can get the Georgia scrum firing on all cylinders in Japan then he may well help them pull off some memorable upsets.

14-10 victory. Nonetheless, Georgia had announced their arrival as an opponent to be feared.

They managed to record a solitary win in New Zealand four years later, but it was in England at the last tournament that they truly began to fulfil their potential. They kicked off their campaign with a 17-10 victory over Tonga, who had been above them in the World Rugby Rankings going into the tournament. Defeats to Argentina and New Zealand followed, but Georgia recovered by sneaking over the line against Namibia to win 17-16.

It meant, for the first time, they had recorded two wins at a Rugby World Cup and, by finishing third in their pool, they also qualified automatically for the next edition in Japan.

This achievement has provided Georgia with the luxury of having four years to prepare for this Rugby World Cup 2019, a new experience for them. Nor has this stopped them from marching to success in the Rugby Europe Championship, one of the qualification paths for the tournament. They claimed the trophy in 2018 and 2019, going unbeaten on both occasions.

After Georgia's superb Rugby World Cup four years ago, head coach Milton Haig is determined to follow up with a strong showing in Japan. They will fancy their chances of success against Pool D rivals Uruguay, but the matches against Australia, Fiji and Wales will be truer tests of just how far they have come.

As ever, the scrum will be crucial to Georgia's chances of success. Despite a population of just 3.7 million, no one produces props quite like the Georgians. They boast some of the best props in the world among their ranks, with several of them playing their club rugby in France.

"We are always in a battle so we love to scrum," prop Davit Zirakashvili explained before the last Rugby World Cup. "The Georgian nature means you never avoid a challenge, never back down."

RUGBY WORLD CUP PERFORMANCES

1987	Did not enter	2003	Pool stage
1991	Did not enter	2007	Pool stage
1995	Did not qualify	2011	Pool stage
1999	Did not qualify	2015	Pool stage

FIJI

Without doubt a favourite among rugby fans all over the world, Fiji always have the potential to pull off the spectacular and unexpected. Among their squad they boast some of the best players on the planet, such as Leone Nakarawa. If they can gel in Japan, they will be a force to be reckoned with.

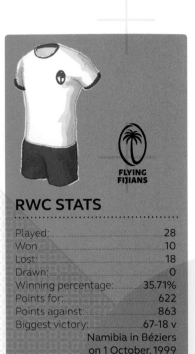

FLYING FIJIANS

RWC STATS

Played:	28
Won	10
Lost:	18
Drawn:	0
Winning percentage:	35.71%
Points for:	622
Points against:	863
Biggest victory:	67-18 v Namibia in Béziers on 1 October, 1999
Heaviest defeat:	66-0 v Wales in Hamilton on 2 October, 2011
World Rugby Ranking:	9

COACH

JOHN McKEE

When he was appointed by Fiji in 2014, John McKee became the country's ninth head coach in 20 years. However, since taking charge, he has brought stability to the role and this is his second Rugby World Cup in charge. McKee has worked hard to improve Fiji's lineout and scrum play, which are areas where they have previously struggled. He led them to four Pacific Nations Cups in a row from 2015-18.

Above: Fiji celebrate their 38-34 victory over Wales at Rugby World Cup 2007.

If you want entertainment when watching rugby, then look no further than Fiji. Of all the teams competing at Rugby World Cup 2019, the Flying Fijians are the most capable of wowing fans with their off-the-cuff attack play. They will run from any part of the pitch, offload out of a tackle when it appears as though no pass is on, and score tries from the tightest of spots using unrivalled pace and power.

However, for all their flair and flamboyance, Fiji have not delivered the goods at Rugby World Cups in terms of their level of talent. At rugby sevens, they are one of the leading sides and they won the gold medal at the Rio Olympics in 2016 when the sport made its debut at the Games.

But in the 15s game, Fiji have, so far, only two quarter-final

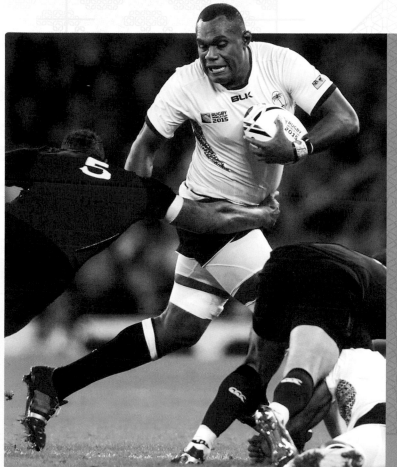

STAR PLAYER

LEONE NAKARAWA

Position:	Second row
Born:	2 April, 1988, Tavua, Fiji
Club:	Racing 92 (FRA)
Height:	1.98m (6ft 6in)
Weight:	125kg (19st 4lb)
Caps:	53
Points:	60 (12t)

Fijian players are renowned for their ability to offload in the tackle and Leone Nakarawa is perhaps the best in the business. With his huge frame, the second row is able to get his arms free and he is a nightmare for defenders. Brilliant in the lineout too and strong in defence, Nakarawa is an all-round performer. He helped Fiji to win the island's first-ever Olympic medal – and it was gold in rugby sevens – at the 2016 Games in Rio, showcasing his deceptively nimble footwork in the process. A star of French club Racing 92, Nakarawa was voted European Player of the Year in 2018. He will take some stopping in Japan.

appearances at Rugby World Cups to cheer about. That is by no means a bad achievement, but a nation with the talent possessed by Fiji should arguably be doing more.

The first of Fiji's trips to the knockout stages came at the inaugural Rugby World Cup in 1987. After coming second in their pool behind eventual winners New Zealand, they set up a quarter-final with France. However, they were defeated by Les Bleus, who went on to make the final.

That first tournament showed signs of promise for Fiji and suggested they would be a threat in the coming years. However, they failed to get out of their pool in 1991, and four years later, they did not even qualify for the Rugby World Cup in South Africa.

A quarter-final play-off in 1999 was an improvement, but four years later came another pool stage exit, and

it was not until 2007 that Fiji roared back onto the international stage. In France, they qualified for the quarter-finals after a stunning 38-34 win over Wales in the pool stages, which showcased the best of Fiji's attacking flair. They were downed 37-20 by South Africa in the quarter-finals, but the rugby world had fallen in love with the Flying Fijians again.

Since then, the last two tournaments have yielded two disappointing pool stage exits. In both 2011 and 2015 Fiji managed just a solitary victory and all six of their defeats were by at least 10 points.

Head coach John McKee knows they must do better in terms of results in Japan. Since taking charge in 2014, he has improved the playing level of the team and they earned a landmark first victory over France in November 2018. However, that good day came just weeks after a 54-17 loss to Scotland, highlighting how Fiji can blow hot and cold.

Despite rising to a best-ever eighth in the World Rugby Rankings in 2018, it is hard to predict how McKee's side will perform in Japan. One thing is for certain: they will be a joy to watch.

RUGBY WORLD CUP PERFORMANCES

1987	Quarter-final	2003	Pool stage
1991	Pool stage	2007	Quarter-final
1995	Did not qualify	2011	Pool stage
1999	Quarter-final play-off	2015	Pool stage

URUGUAY

Rugby World Cup 2019 will be Uruguay's fourth tournament, and they will be hoping to give a strong account of themselves after a winless time in England four years ago. A promising qualification journey, which culminated in victory over Canada, is an indication of how they are continuing to improve.

STATS

Played:	11
Won	2
Lost:	9
Drawn:	0
Winning percentage:	18.18%
Points for:	128
Points against:	578
Biggest victory:	27-15 v Spain in Galashiels on 2 October, 1999
Heaviest defeat:	111-13 v England in Brisbane on 2 November, 2003
World Rugby Ranking:	16

COACH

ESTEBAN MENESES
Placed in charge of Uruguay after Pablo Lemoine stepped down in December 2016, Esteban Meneses has gone about his work in impressive fashion after being recommended for the role by the then Argentina head coach, Daniel Hourcade. Meneses, a flanker in his playing days, had never coached an international side before this. However, he led Uruguay to Rugby World Cup qualification with a 70-60 aggregate victory over Canada in the two-leg play-off.

Above: Uruguay have come a long way from their debut at Rugby World Cup 1999.

The Uruguay side that will grace the field in Japan at Rugby World Cup 2019 is a far cry from the team that made the country's tournament debut back in 1999.

Rugby may have been moving into the professional era back then, but Uruguay's squad was still made up entirely of amateur players. It meant they faced a difficult task during the tournament in Wales, but they gave a good account of themselves.

A victory in their opening match against fellow amateurs Spain sparked wild celebrations and their coach at the time, Daniel Herrera, could barely hold back his emotions. "It's like being world champions," he said. "It's almost a miracle for a country like ours to be here." Defeats to powerhouses Scotland and South Africa followed, but no one could take away Uruguay's first-ever Rugby World Cup victory.

Four years later they were back for more

STAR PLAYER

JUAN MANUEL GAMINARA

Position:	Flanker
Born:	1 May, 1989, Montevideo, Uruguay
Club:	Old Boys (URU)
Height:	1.75m (5ft 9in)
Weight:	95kg (14st 13lb)
Caps:	64
Points:	30 (6t)

The fact that Juan Manuel Gaminara's nickname is "Garrafa" (gas tank) should tell you all you need to know about his style of play. The flanker is full of energy and running, and his work rate around the pitch is one of the reasons why he is Uruguay's captain. Few players cover as much ground as he does and his work ethic is unrivalled. A key part of his country's play-off wins over Canada that booked their place in Japan, Gaminara will be playing in his second Rugby World Cup; having played all but 15 minutes of the four matches in England four years ago.

after qualifying for the tournament in Australia. Again, Uruguay showed signs of promise as they kept up their record of securing at least one win at every Rugby World Cup. This time victory came against Georgia as they ran out 24-12 winners in Sydney.

They missed out on the next two Rugby World Cups, though, as defeats to Portugal and Romania in the repechage denied them spots at the 2007 and 2011 editions of the tournament.

Victory over Russia meant Uruguay secured the final spot at Rugby World Cup 2015, but it turned out to be a difficult time. Drawn in a pool with Australia, England, Fiji and Wales they failed to secure a win at the tournament for the first time.

They still battled hard in every match, although all four defeats were by more than 30 points. It did showcase how far they have

come since their debut in 1999. The amateur side of then is starting to fade, and now an increasing number of their players play professionally overseas. A High Performance Centre has also been formed in Montevideo and there is belief that greater success could be coming in the future.

The current crop of players will certainly be hoping to secure a victory in Japan after an impressive qualifying campaign. For Rugby World Cup 2015, Uruguay were the last team to qualify – but this time around they booked their spot in

Japan more than 18 months before the start of the tournament.

A 70-60 two-legged defeat of Canada in a play-off was enough to do that. The first leg victory, 38-29 in Vancouver, was Uruguay's first over the Canucks on Canadian soil. Carrying a nine-point advantage, they sealed the deal in the second leg in Montevideo a week later. Success in the match came after Canada missed a last-kick conversion, giving Uruguay a 32-31 win. Qualification sparked wild celebrations in Montevideo. Any victory in Japan would surely cause similar scenes of jubilation.

RUGBY WORLD CUP PERFORMANCES

1987	Did not enter	2003	Pool stage
1991	Did not enter	2007	Did not qualify
1995	Did not qualify	2011	Did not qualify
1999	Pool stage	2015	Pool stage

FRANCE FIGHT BACK TO STUN NEW ZEALAND

6 October, 2007: Millennium Stadium, Cardiff

After an opening round defeat to Argentina at Rugby World Cup 2007, hosts France were under pressure to rediscover their form for their quarter-final with New Zealand. By contrast, the All Blacks had never failed to make the semi-finals, and had topped their pool with four wins. They started brightly too, opening up a 13-0 lead after 31 minutes. Just before the break, however, France grabbed a lifeline when fly-half Lionel Beauxis slotted a penalty. There was now light at the end of the tunnel for Les Bleus and a spirited second-half fightback was completed when Yannick Jauzion scored with 11 minutes to go. His try levelled the match and Jean-Baptiste Élissalde coolly slotted the conversion to secure a memorable 20-18 win for France.

Right: New Zealand players were left stunned as France pulled off an amazing comeback to knock them out of Rugby World Cup 2007.

![RUGBY WORLD CUP™ JAPAN日本2019]

THE STARS TO WATCH

Ever since the first Rugby World Cup in 1987, the tournament has provided the perfect stage for players to showcase their talent at the highest level of all. Over the years, the likes of David Campese, Jonah Lomu, Jonny Wilkinson, Richie McCaw and many others have seized the opportunity to etch their name into the game's history books. Rugby World Cup 2019 promises to be no different and the following players could be the ones making their mark in Japan.

Left: Michael Leitch can rubber-stamp his sporting hero status by helping Japan progress in 2019.

All player statistics correct at 18 March, 2019

Beauden
BARRETT

Since Rugby World Cup 2015, no player's star has risen quite like that of Beauden Barrett. The fly-half has become one of the current game's greatest players and he is all set to take Japan by storm. Quick in body and mind, and with an exceedingly high skill level, he is one of the most exciting players to watch.

FACTS AND FIGURES

Born:	27 May, 1991, New Plymouth, New Zealand
Position:	Fly-half
Club:	Hurricanes (NZL)
Height:	1.87m (6ft 2in)
Weight:	91kg (14st 4lb)
Caps:	73
Debut:	v Ireland in Hamilton on 23 June, 2012
Points:	595 (32t, 138c, 51p, 2dg)

When Dan Carter retired from international rugby after Rugby World Cup 2015, everyone was wondering who would step into the great man's number 10 jersey.

Aaron Cruden looked like the frontrunner, while Lima Sopoaga was lurking on the fringes. Beauden Barrett was a candidate too. He had finished the 2014 Super Rugby season with 209 points for his club side Hurricanes – more than any other New Zealander.

Barrett had also caught the eye at Rugby World Cup 2015, coming off the bench to fill in at wing and full-back.

He even managed a try in the final.

It was Cruden, though, who got the first crack at replacing Carter, but when he was injured against Wales during the second test of the June series in 2016, Barrett took his chance.

He came off the bench to score 11 points and then, after starting the final test, he weighed in with 26 points in a 46-6 win.

Barrett has made the number 10 jersey his own since then, and he capped off a defining 2016 by helping New Zealand win the Rugby Championship with six wins from six. The All Blacks fly-half was the

competition's top points scorer with 81 – a total that was 28 more than the next best.

Barrett's rise has continued since then. In 2017, he was the series' leading points scorer with 41 for New Zealand's three tests with the British and Irish Lions. He notched a further 70 as, again, the All Blacks won the Rugby Championship with a perfect record.

The year was rounded off for Barrett when he retained World Rugby's Player of the Year award, an accolade he had first won in 2016. It was a feat that had been achieved only once previously, by another All Black great: Richie McCaw.

Above: Beauden Barrett capped off a memorable Rugby World Cup in 2015 by scoring in the final.

Jonathan
DAVIES

An unbeaten tourist with the British and Irish Lions in Australia and New Zealand, Jonathan Davies has established himself as one of the best centres in the world. A Six Nations Grand Slam winner with Wales too, he will now be hoping for more success at Rugby World Cup 2019.

FACTS AND FIGURES

Born:	5 April, 1988, Solihill, England
Position:	Centre
Club:	Scarlets (WAL)
Height:	1.85m (6ft 1in)
Weight:	101kg (15st 12lb)
Caps:	73 (+6 Lions)
Debut:	v Canada in Toronto on 30 May, 2009
Points:	75 (15t)

Born in Solihull, England, Jonathan Davies moved back to Wales with his Welsh parents when he was just six months old.

It was there that the centre grew up and began his rugby education at primary school in the village of Bancyfelin in Carmarthenshire, while his parents ran the Fox & Hounds pub. No guesses why Davies' nickname is "Fox".

From an early age his talent was clear to see, and at the age of just 18 he was making his debut for Scarlets. Unsurprisingly, international recognition duly followed and in May 2009 Davies made his debut for Wales against Canada.

The centre has continued a steady rise since then and he goes into this Rugby World Cup having featured at the 2011 tournament, though he missed Rugby World Cup 2015 through injury.

Davies also has two British and Irish Lions series under his belt, touring with them in 2013 and 2017. The latter of those proved to be a landmark moment for the outside centre as he was named Player of the Series by his team-mates for his efforts in New Zealand.

A serious foot injury in November 2017 while playing for Wales against Argentina cruelly dented his progression and forced him to miss the 2018 Six Nations.

Davies will be itching to make his mark in Japan and he has the potential to be one of the stars of the tournament.

While incredibly strong and powerful, Davies is much more than the classic crash-ball centre. His quick hands can help unlock defences and he is more than capable of jinking around players – instead of running over them.

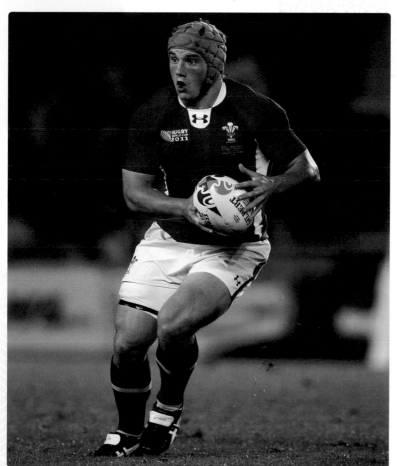

Above: Jonathan Davies is set to play in his second Rugby World Cup as he bids for glory.

Owen
FARRELL

Once the youngest player to play in English professional rugby union, Owen Farrell has never looked back. He was just 17 years and 11 days old when he turned out for Saracens in October 2008. Now a key part of England's backline, whether he plays at fly-half or inside centre, he will be crucial to their chances in Japan.

FACTS AND FIGURES

Born: 24 September, 1991, Billinge, England
Position: ....Fly-half
Club: ....Saracens (ENG)
Height: 1.88m (6ft 2in)
Weight: 92kg (14st 7lb)
Caps: ....70 (+4 Lions)
Debut: ..v Scotland at Murrayfield, Edinburgh, on 4 February, 2012
Points: 785 (10t, 120c, 162p, 3dg)

Ever since Owen Farrell broke onto the scene as a teenager, it has been clear he was destined to go right to the top.

The fly-half, who can also operate in the centres, has always shown composure and maturity way above his years, and he is now a key leader in the England team.

Farrell made his debut for England back in 2012 and enjoyed a memorable 12 months that culminated in him being nominated for World Rugby Player of the Year.

Since then he has become a pivotal part of the England backline, with his goal-kicking also making him a valuable asset to the team. Indeed, Farrell succeeded with 16 out of 18 attempts at goal at Rugby World Cup 2015.

That tournament ultimately ended in disappointment for Farrell and his team-mates, but he was the key cog in their march to the Six Nations Grand Slam in 2016.

Farrell was the competition's top points scorer, with 69, and even filled in as captain for the injured Dylan Hartley, a role he has undertaken when called upon.

Farrell was nominated for World Rugby Player of the Year in 2016 and 2017 and he has continued to excel for both club and country.

Now rightly considered one of the best players on the planet, he will be instrumental to England's hopes of success in Japan. His ability to perform under immense pressure at crucial moments is what makes Farrell stand out from the rest, and England will need him to stand up and lead them at Rugby World Cup 2019.

Above: A leader for England and a fierce competitor, Owen Farrell is set to shine in Japan.

Will GENIA

After coming off the bench to make his debut for Australia back in 2009, against New Zealand, Will Genia has never looked back. He has gone on to earn a century of caps for his country, cementing his position as one of the best scrum-halves to ever play the game.

FACTS AND FIGURES

Born: 17 January, 1988, Port Moresby, Papua New Guinea
Position: Scrum-half
Club: Melbourne Rebels (AUS)
Height: 1.74m (5ft 9in)
Weight: 82kg (12st 12lb)
Caps: 100
Debut: v New Zealand in Auckland on 18 July, 2009
Points: 90 (18t)

If Eddie Jones is to be believed, Will Genia's rise to the top has not come easy. Jones may now be preparing England for Rugby World Cup 2019 in Japan, but he can still remember first setting eyes on Genia when he was coming through the ranks of the Queensland Reds more than a decade ago.

"I remember this fat little bloke in the academy," said Jones. "They said: 'Nah he doesn't work hard enough.'

"We had a bit of a chat about what he needed to do and where he needed to go and I never saw a boy work as hard as him. It's a real tribute to him how hard he's worked and what a great player he's been for Australia."

Genia has gone on to earn 100 caps for the Wallabies and he is in esteemed company given that George Gregan is the only other scrum-half to achieve such a feat.

After breaking into the Australia team in 2009, Genia cemented his position as first choice in 2010, and by the following year he was an integral part of the side at Rugby World Cup 2011. He even captained the Wallabies against the USA in Wellington.

By 2013, the scrum-half had already amassed 50 caps and two years later he shone as Australia made it all the way to the final of Rugby World Cup 2015. New Zealand broke Wallaby hearts that day, but Genia will be hoping for a strong showing in Japan.

Australia have been unable to reach the heights they showed in England four years ago since the last tournament, but the big stage often brings out the best in them. And, if they are to shine, Genia will be key to their chances.

Above: After winning a semi-final in 2015, Genia is looking to go one better in Japan.

Stuart
HOGG

After bursting onto the scene for Scotland as a teenager, Stuart Hogg has matured to become one of the most lethal full-backs in rugby. Blessed with electric pace and an abundance of creativity, he will undoubtedly cause plenty of problems for defences during the tournament in Japan.

FACTS AND FIGURES

Born:	24 June, 1992, Melrose, Scotland
Position:	Full-back
Club:	Glasgow Warriors (SCO)
Height:	1.80m (5ft 11in)
Weight:	93kg (14st 9lb)
Caps:	67
Debut:	v Wales at Millennium Stadium, Cardiff, on 12 February, 2012
Points:	107 (19t, 4p)

After suffering the pain of a last-minute quarter-final defeat to Australia at Rugby World Cup 2015, Stuart Hogg will be out to make his mark in Japan. The full-back's star has soared since the last tournament in England and he has been in stunning form.

Named Player of the Championship for the 2016 and 2017 Six Nations, Hogg has developed his game even further to have more weapons in his arsenal. Always capable of a brilliant solo try, the full-back has now become a creative spark who can put others over the whitewash too.

From a young age, Hogg's talent has been clear and he was handed his debut for club side Glasgow Warriors at just 18. Just one year later and he made his Scotland bow during the 2012 Six Nations, coming on as a substitute against Wales after 16 minutes for the injured Max Evans.

Hogg's versatility led to him being deployed at fly-half, centre and wing as he continued his development, but it is at full-back where he has cemented his place in the Scotland team.

Despite his age, he has already been called up to two British and Irish Lions tours. The second of those, in 2017, was cruelly cut short early due to injury, which denied Hogg the chance to showcase his talent in the test matches against New Zealand.

He will now be hoping that Rugby World Cup 2019 in Japan provides the perfect stage to underline what a talent he has become.

Above: Stuart Hogg will be one of the most exciting players to watch in Japan and crucial to Scotland's chances of success.

Michael
LEITCH

Captain for Japan's memorable win over South Africa at Rugby World Cup 2015, Michael Leitch will be hoping to create more magical memories in Japan. A tireless flanker who often finishes matches with the highest tackle count, he is the embodiment of the Brave Blossoms' incredible work ethic.

FACTS AND FIGURES

Born:	7 October, 1988, Christchurch, New Zealand
Position:	Flanker
Club:	Sunwolves (JPN)
Height:	1.90m (6ft 3in)
Weight:	105kg (16st 7lb)
Caps:	59
Debut:	v USA in Nagoya on 16 November, 2008
Points:	85 (17t)

Michael Leitch was born in New Zealand to a Kiwi father and a Fijian mother, and followed an unlikely path to become captain of Japan. The flanker spent much of his childhood in Christchurch and attended St. Bede's College.

However, at the age of 15 he headed to Japan to study – and he has never looked back. Leitch spent three years at high school, and then moved to Tokai University. After two years there, he had caught the eye of then Japan coach John Kirwan.

The flanker was made captain for the World Rugby U20 Championship in 2008 and that same year, aged just 20, he made his senior debut for Japan.

Leitch has immersed himself in Japanese culture, to the point where he now claims he speaks the native language better than English. He has certainly become a key cog of the team, and Rugby World Cup 2019 will be his third tournament.

Leitch was one of Japan's best players at the 2011 competition, while he captained the side superbly to three wins four years later. The flanker was particularly impressive in the historic victory over South Africa, topping the tackle count with 17 and also scoring a try.

Crucially, Leitch also snubbed the chance for a kickable penalty in the dying moments as Japan went for the win instead of a draw. It was a brave decision – and it paid off. The Brave Blossoms' fans will be dreaming of more of the same this time around in their own backyard.

Above: No one epitomises the Brave Blossoms more than their captain and leader Michael Leitch.

Malcolm
MARX

South Africa have a proud history of developing world-class hookers and Malcolm Marx is the latest in a long line to impress in the famous Springbok jersey. An explosive ball carrier, who is also highly effective at the breakdown, Marx looks set to be one of the stars of Rugby World Cup 2019.

FACTS AND FIGURES

Born:	13 July, 1994, Germiston, South Africa
Position:	Hooker
Club:	Lions (RSA)
Height:	1.89m (6ft 2in)
Weight:	112kg (17st 9lb)
Caps:	24
Debut:	v New Zealand in Christchurch on 17 September, 2016
Points:	20 (4t)

If any hooker sums up how the position has developed in the modern era of rugby, it is Malcolm Marx. At a height of 1.89m and weighing 112kg, he is a phenomenal athlete, who has burst onto the scene with devastating effect.

In 2016 Marx was handed his South Africa debut, coming off the bench to face New Zealand. This was a baptism of fire for the youngster, then aged just 22, but he has grown ever since.

The following year proved to be a decisive one and he made the number two jersey his own. He was named man of the match for his performance in the first of three tests against France, while he excelled during the Rugby Championship too.

Marx finished a stunning 2017 by being named SA Rugby Player of the Year and retaining the award of SA Rugby Young Player of the Year – which he won in 2016.

Not content with shining for South Africa, the hooker has been excelling at club level with the Lions. He finished the 2018 Super Rugby season with 12 tries to his name – only four fewer than top scorer Ben Lam.

On top of that, Marx had a lineout success rate of 89.2 per cent in the same competition, while only one player bettered his tally of 27 turnovers.

The hooker's incredible statistics for tries and turnovers have helped make him one of the game's best forwards. Few can break tackles like he does or get over the ball so effectively at the breakdown. Japan looks like the perfect stage for his star to continue rising.

Above: Still young in rugby terms , this should be the first of many Rugby World Cups for Malcolm Marx.

Sergio
PARISSE

After making his debut for Italy at the age of 18, Sergio Parisse has gone on to become his country's most capped player. The number eight is Italy's captain and talisman, and he will have a crucial role to play if they are to go far at Rugby World Cup 2019.

FACTS AND FIGURES

Born: 12 September, 1983, La Plata, Argentina
Position: Number eight
Club: Stade Français (FRA)
Height: 1.96m (6ft 5in)
Weight: 112kg (17st 8lb)
Caps: 138
Debut: v New Zealand in Hamilton on 8 June, 2002
Points: 78 (15t, 1dg)

Sergio Parisse may have been born in Argentina, but cut the number eight open and you will see he bleeds the blue of Italy.

His father, Sergio Snr, played for one of the oldest clubs in Italy, L'Aquila, before his work with Alitalia meant he was posted to La Plata.

It was there that Sergio Jnr was born and raised, but the family never forgot their roots. Italian was still spoken at home, and holidays were often spent in Italy.

Parisse's talent was clear for all to see and by the age of 18 he was being handed his test debut against New Zealand in Hamilton. A year later he was scoring his first try for his country against Canada at Rugby World Cup 2003.

His form at club level for Italian side Treviso was not going unnoticed either, which prompted Stade Français to swoop for him in 2005.

By the age of 24, he already had 50 caps to his name and he was duly made captain of his country in 2008. That same year, Parisse became the first Italian to be nominated for World Rugby Player of the Year. He was nominated again in 2013.

Multilingual and multi-talented, Parisse has established himself as one of the all-time great number eights. His handling ability rivals that of any back, while his vision makes him lethal in attack – out wide or in a tight space. Parisse is a giant of a player, who will go down as one of the game's greats.

Above: The heartbeat of the Italy team and one of the best number eights in history, Japan could be Sergio Parisse's last hurrah.

Louis
PICAMOLES

When it comes to imposing and powerful forwards, there are few in the world who can match Louis Picamoles. The number eight is one of the most feared players on the planet when running with the ball in hand due to his ability to break tackles and offload to team-mates. He will be a key weapon for France in Japan.

FACTS AND FIGURES

Born:	5 February, 1986, Paris, France
Position:	Number eight
Club:	Montpellier (FRA)
Height:	1.92m (6ft 4in)
Weight:	116kg (256lb)
Caps:	77
Debut:	v Ireland in Paris on 9 February, 2008
Points:	50 (10t)

A look back at the history of Louis Picamoles' nicknames tells you all you need to know about how highly rated he is by those in the game.

Let's start with his most common one, "King Louis", in part given to him because of his French roots, but also because of his presence on the pitch.

Picamoles is a talismanic figure, someone who stands tall in the tackle and is ready to go toe to toe with any opponent. When the match gets physical, he gets going and that can be a unifying effect for all involved.

Then there was the nickname Picamoles inherited during his one season with Northampton Saints over the course of the 2016-17 campaign. He may have only spent a year there but within weeks his team-mates were all calling him "Iceberg". With such a low centre of gravity it was claimed tackling him in training was like hitting the top of an iceberg - you barely made a dent.

For all his strength and power, and undeniable talent, Picamoles has not always performed for France. Indeed, throughout his career he has dropped in and out of the squad under various coaches.

Under current head coach Jacques Brunel he is becoming a key part of the squad, though, with his experience proving to be a valuable asset. Crucially, Picamoles also gives France the ability to get over the gain line when opposition defences can be tough to break through.

The forward may be coming towards the latter stages of his career, but he still remains a threat and on his day he is simply unplayable. If he shines in Japan, France will too.

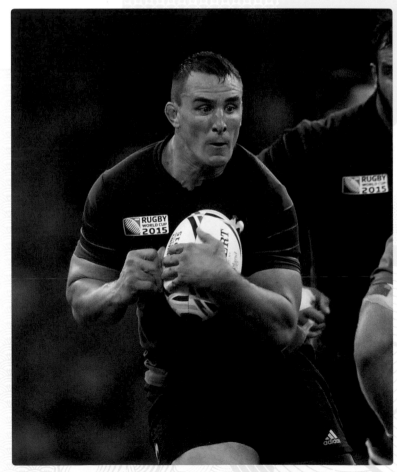

Above: Barnstorming back-row forward Louis Picamoles is back for his third Rugby World Cup.

Semi
RADRADRA

Semi Radradra may have only made his Fiji debut in 2018, but he has already established himself as a key player for his country. Previously a star of Rugby League, the wing switched codes in 2017 and he has not looked back since. Radradra is certainly one to watch in Japan.

FACTS AND FIGURES

Born:	13 June, 1992, Suva, Fiji
Position:	Centre
Club:	Bordeaux-Bègles (FRA)
Height:	1.90m (6ft 3in)
Weight:	105kg (16st 7lb)
Caps:	3
Debut:	v Georgia in Suav on 16 June, 2018
Points:	15 (3t)

The fact that Semi Radradra's nickname is 'Semi-Trailer' tells you all you need to know about the talented centre: the term is usually used to describe a type of truck.

Standing at 1.90m and weighing in at 105kg, Radradra has the ability to run over his opponents if he so wishes. However that should not take away from his electric pace and nimble footwork, which has made him a nightmare for defences. The Fijian really is a dual threat of pace and power.

It was in rugby sevens that Radradra first caught people's attention. He shone for Fiji at the Dubai Sevens in 2011 and two years later he was making a name for himself in Rugby League for Australian side Parramatta Eels.

The centre was nothing short of a phenomenon, and he finished his time there in 2017 after scoring 82 tries in 94 National Rugby League matches.

Given his success, Radradra's decision to leave the Parramatta Eels was tough but the chance to switch codes and sign for French club Toulon was too big a pull to turn down.

He has since joined Bordeaux-Bègles, while also being capped by Fiji. His debut for the Flying Fijians came in 2018 and he scored a try against Georgia to mark it.

Another try followed during a defeat to Scotland, before he capped off a brilliant start to his international career by scoring in Fiji's historic 21-14 win over France in November.

That, though, is surely just the start for a talent like Radradra.

Below: Semi Radradra has adapted quickly since switching codes.

Nicolás
SÁNCHEZ

The top points scorer at Rugby World Cup 2015, Nicolás Sánchez has continued his development to become one of the best fly-halves on the planet. A creative and lethal playmaker, who can create space for others, he is also deadly accurate with his boot too.

FACTS AND FIGURES

Born:	26 October, 1988, San Miguel de Tucumán, Argentina
Position:	Fly-half
Club:	Stade Français (FRA)
Height:	1.77m (5ft 10in)
Weight:	83kg (183lb)
Caps:	74
Debut:	v Uruguay in Santiago on 21 May, 2010
Points:	709 (11t, 99c, 140p, 12dg)

When Argentina arrived at Rugby World Cup 2015, many were expecting the great Juan Martín Hernández to steal the show. For years "El Mago", the Magician, had been the Pumas' creative force and chief playmaker on the field.

However, come the end of the tournament, it was Nicolás Sánchez who was rightly grabbing all the headlines. The fly-half was outstanding in England, finishing with 97 points to his name and helping Argentina reach the semi-finals.

Ever since then, Sánchez's importance to Los Pumas has only grown and he has developed into one of the best fly-halves in the world.

He managed 99 points over the course of 2016 and 2017 Rugby Championships, despite Argentina claiming only one win during that time.

Last year was a decisive one for both Sánchez and Los Pumas. Once again the fly-half sparkled in the Rugby Championship and ended as the tournament's top points scorer.

Argentina's form improved too as they claimed two victories, including a 23-19 win over the Wallabies in Australia – their first victory over the hosts on Australian soil for 35 years.

An unlikely double over Australia could have been secured because they led 31-7 at half-time in the home match, only for the Wallabies to roar back and win 45-34.

After he signed for Stade Français for the 2018-19 season, the fear was that Sánchez's Argentina career could be over due to restrictions regarding overseas players.

However, head coach Mario Ledesma was given permission to select those playing abroad in extreme cases. Sánchez is certainly that.

Left: Deadly from the kicking tee and dangerous with the ball in hand, when Nicolás Sánchez performs, so do Argentina.

Johnny
SEXTON

A European champion at club level, a two-time tourist with the British and Irish Lions and a Six Nations Grand Slam winner, Johnny Sexton will be hoping to fire Ireland all the way at Rugby World Cup 2019. And, if the men in green are to go far, the fly-half will have a key role to play.

FACTS AND FIGURES

Born:	11 July, 1985, Dublin, Ireland
Position:	Fly-half
Club:	Leinster (IRE)
Height:	1.88m (6ft 2in)
Weight:	92kg (14st 6lb)
Caps:	83 (+6 Lions)
Debut:	v Fiji in Dublin on 21 November, 2009
Points:	761 (10t, 99c, 167p, 4dg)

When Johnny Sexton stepped up to command the match as Leinster won their first European Cup in 2009 with a 19-16 win over Leicester Tigers, it finally dawned on everyone just how special a player he was.

Thrown in because of an injury to the team's usual fly-half, Felipe Contepomi, the then 23-year-old ran the game and capped off his performance with a drop goal from the halfway line and the match-winning penalty with 10 minutes to go. He hasn't looked back since.

Sexton has excelled for club and country since the last Rugby World Cup, when Ireland were knocked out in the quarter-finals.

The fly-half played a key role in helping Ireland win a third Grand Slam in 2018. Joe Schmidt's side conquered all before them in the Six Nations and Sexton's 83rd-minute drop goal, after 41 phases set the tone, enabling them to claim an opening round, 15-13 victory away to France.

Sexton finished the competition with 44 points and was duly nominated for Player of the Championship, although that honour went to team-mate Jacob Stockdale.

This was followed by a first series win away to Australia since 1979, during which Sexton scored 31 points, and it capped off a stunning 2017-18 season that saw him undefeated as a starter for Ireland and Leinster.

He is undoubtedly one of the most creative fly-halves on the planet.

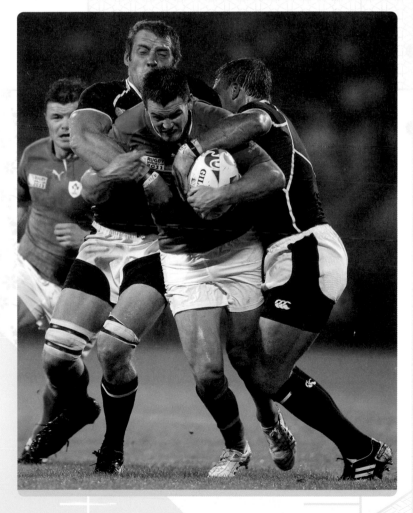

Right: The World Rugby Player of the Year 2018, Johnny Sexton hopes to take Ireland all the way in Japan.

CARTER IS FINALLY KING OF THE WORLD

31 October, 2015: Twickenham, London

Ahead of Rugby World Cup 2011, Dan Carter had been tipped as the star of the tournament. However, injury during the pool stages of the competition forced the fly-half to watch from the sidelines as the All Blacks were crowned world champions. Four years later in England, Carter was determined to make amends and he got his chance as New Zealand once again made the final. This time Australia were standing in their way but, guided by Carter, the All Blacks rose to the occasion. The fly-half was in imperious form, scoring 19 points and picking up the man of the match award as New Zealand won 34-17. The pain of four years ago had been erased and Carter was truly a Rugby World Cup winner.

RUGBY WORLD CUP™
JAPAN 日本 2019

RUGBY WORLD CUP
HISTORY

Ever since the first tournament in 1987, Rugby World Cup has been the pinnacle for all those competing in the sport. Each tournament has been full of drama as the very best teams on the planet fight to lift the Webb Ellis Cup. Over the course of the eight Rugby World Cups so far, four different countries have been crowned world champions – but no one has been a bigger winner than the game itself.

Right: David Campese lifts the Webb Ellis Cup after Australia's 12-6 victory over England in the final of Rugby World Cup 1991 at Twickenham.

RUGBY WORLD CUP 1987
New Zealand and Australia

They were joint hosts of the inaugural Rugby World Cup, so the pressure was on New Zealand and Australia to go all the way. In the end, it was the All Blacks who came out on top as they defeated France in the final in front of a packed Eden Park crowd.

If New Zealand and Australia were feeling the pressure of being hosts of the first-ever Rugby World Cup, they certainly did not show it.

Both sides cruised through the pool stages and it was the All Blacks in particular who looked in formidable form. They amassed 190 points from their three victories to book a place in the quarter-finals alongside Fiji, who sneaked through from Pool 3 ahead of Italy and Argentina on tries scored.

Like New Zealand, Australia made the perfect start as they qualified top of Pool 1 with a 100 per cent record. A 19-6 victory over England, who finished second, was the highlight of a pool stage that saw them score more than 100 points.

Away from the hosts, Wales were proving that they were contenders to go all the way with a bright start to the tournament. A hard-fought 13-6 victory over Ireland got them on their way and wins over Tonga (29-16) and Canada (40-9) ensured they qualified as winners of Pool 2. Ireland recovered from their opening round disappointment to finish second.

The line-up for the knockout stages was completed by France and Scotland, who finished level on points in Pool 4.

The pair played out a brilliant 20-20 draw to kick off their campaigns, and both followed it up with wins over Romania and Zimbabwe.

France, in the end, secured top spot on points difference, which meant that Scotland had to face the imperious All Blacks.

Scotland proved to be no match for New Zealand, who carried on their fine form from the pool stages with a 30-3 victory.

France's reward for finishing first was an encounter with Fiji and they ran in four tries on their way to a 31-16 victory.

Awaiting them would be the winner of Australia and Ireland's match, which took place in Sydney. Backed by a home crowd and the boot of Michael Lynagh, the Wallabies progressed after a 33-15 victory.

Wales set up a semi-final showdown with New Zealand after defeating England in their quarter-final. Gareth Roberts, Robert Jones and John Devereux all scored tries as the Welsh claimed an impressive 16-3 win.

Their run ended there as, like so many before them, they could not topple New Zealand. The All Blacks ran in eight tries on their way to a 49-6 victory that ensured they would have the chance to win the Rugby World Cup in their own backyard.

RUGBY WORLD CUP HEROES

DAVID KIRK (New Zealand)

Behind any great rugby team is a great captain, and David Kirk was pivotal to New Zealand's success in 1987. Blessed with brilliant intelligence on the field, Kirk marshalled his team superbly from scrum-half throughout the tournament. His speed around the park and precision passing made him a thorn in any defence's side and he helped unleash the talented backs outside him such as Craig Green, Grant Fox and John Kirwan.

Standing in their way would be France, who beat Australia 30-24 in their semi-final courtesy of a stunning last-minute try from Serge Blanco. The France full-back completed a brilliant team move to break Australian hearts, who were disappointed again days later as Wales defeated them 22-21 in the bronze final.

For their fellow hosts New Zealand, however, the tournament ended in joy as they won the first-ever Rugby World Cup. Tries from captain David Kirk, Michael Jones and John Kirwan helped them beat France 29-9 in the final in front of 48,000 fans at Eden Park. For Les Bleus it looked as if the final had been just one step too far.

Right: France full-back Serge Blanco finishes off a memorable try to beat hosts Australia in the dying moments of the semi-final.

TOURNAMENT STATISTICS

Host nations – New Zealand and Australia
Dates – 22 May-20 June, 1987
Teams: 16
Matches: 32
Overall attendance: 448,318

POOL 1	W	D	L	PF	PA	Pts
Australia	3	0	0	108	4	6
England	2	0	1	100	32	4
USA	1	0	2	39	99	2
Japan	0	0	3	48	123	0

POOL 2	W	D	L	PF	PA	Pts
Wales	3	0	0	82	31	6
Ireland	2	0	1	84	41	4
Canada	1	0	2	65	90	2
Tonga	0	0	3	29	98	0

POOL 3	W	D	L	PF	PA	Pts
New Zealand	3	0	0	190	34	6
Fiji	1	0	2	56	101	2
Italy	1	0	2	40	110	2
Argentina	1	0	2	49	90	2

POOL 4	W	D	L	PF	PA	Pts
France	2	1	0	145	44	5
Scotland	2	1	0	135	69	5
Romania	1	0	2	61	130	2
Zimbabwe	0	0	3	53	151	0

QUARTER-FINALS

New Zealand	30-3	Scotland
Australia	33-15	Ireland
France	31-16	Fiji
Wales	16-3	England

SEMI-FINALS

France	30-24	Australia
New Zealand	49-6	Wales

BRONZE FINAL

Wales	22-21	Australia

THE FINAL

New Zealand	29-9	France

	NEW ZEALAND	FRANCE
T:	Jones, Kirk, Kirwan	Berbizier
C:	Fox	Camberabero
P:	Fox 4	Camberabero
DG:	Fox	

LEADING POINTS SCORERS
1. 126 Grant Fox (NZL)
2. 82 Michael Lynagh (AUS)
3. 62 Gavin Hastings (SCO)

LEADING TRY SCORERS
1. 6 Craig Green (NZL)
2. 6 John Kirwan (NZL)
3. 5 Matt Burke (AUS)
= 5 Mike Harrison (ENG)
= 5 John Gallagher (NZL)
= 5 Alan Whetton (NZL)
= 5 David Kirk (NZL)

RUGBY WORLD CUP 1991
The UK, Ireland and France

Once again 16 teams came together for the Rugby World Cup as England, France, Ireland, Scotland and Wales all hosted matches. Unlike four years earlier, eight of the sides competing earned a place through qualifying as the competitive nature of the tournament stepped up another level. Shocks and drama swiftly followed.

The rise of emerging rugby nations was a familiar theme at the tournament in 1991 as the game began to grow around the world.

Four years earlier, Wales had finished third, but they were stunned in their very first match by Western Samoa, who pulled off an incredible 16-13 win in Cardiff.

The Western Samoans followed that by narrowly losing 9-3 to Australia, who finished top of Pool C after seeing off Argentina and Wales too.

The Welsh defeats against Australia and Western Samoa meant they were out of the tournament before the knockout stages, but there were more shocks to come.

In Pool D, Canada followed Western Samoa's lead and booked a place in the quarter-finals by finishing second to France – and ahead of Fiji and Romania.

The other side of the draw progressed in a more expected manner as reigning champions New Zealand made a perfect start by winning all three of their Pool A matches. Hosts England followed them into the knockout stages thanks to wins over Italy and USA.

Pool B had a familiar look to it at the end too as Scotland claimed top spot and Ireland finished runners-up. There was some joy for Japan, though, as they claimed a first-ever Rugby World Cup win, beating Zimbabwe 52-8.

After starring in the pool stages, all eyes were on Western Samoa to see if they could continue their heroics. However, Scotland proved too strong for them and roared into the semi-finals in front of 54,000 fans at Murrayfield. Canada's fairytale ended too just a day later as New Zealand showed their might to overcome them 29-13.

Canada and Western Samoa's dreams may have been brought to an end, but England's were still alive and well as they defeated France in Paris. Rory Underwood and Will Carling both scored tries as England marched on with a 19-10 victory that gave them reason for optimism.

The last of the quarter-finals between Australia and Ireland proved to be the most dramatic.

RUGBY WORLD CUP
HEROES

DAVID CAMPESE (Australia)

There are a few finer sights in the history of rugby than David Campese running down the wing. He was the star of Rugby World Cup 1991, finishing as the tournament's joint top try scorer with six. Famed for his creation of the Goose Step, Campese was at times unplayable in a tournament where Australia were crowned world champions. Ireland fly-half Tony Ward neatly summed him up: "He is the Maradona, the Pelé of international rugby, all rolled into one."

TOURNAMENT STATISTICS

Host nations: England, France, Ireland, Scotland and Wales

Dates: 3 October–2 November, 1991

Teams: 16 (33 during qualifying)

Matches: 32

Overall attendance: 1,060,065

POOL A	W	D	L	PF	PA	Pts
New Zealand	3	0	0	95	39	6
England	2	0	1	85	33	4
Italy	1	0	2	57	76	2
USA	0	0	3	24	113	0

POOL B	W	D	L	PF	PA	Pts
Scotland	3	0	0	122	36	6
Ireland	2	0	1	102	51	4
Japan	1	0	2	77	87	2
Zimbabwe	0	0	3	31	158	0

POOL C	W	D	L	PF	PA	Pts
Australia	3	0	0	79	25	6
Western Samoa	2	0	1	54	34	4
Wales	1	0	2	32	61	2
Argentina	0	0	3	38	83	0

POOL D	W	D	L	PF	PA	Pts
France	3	0	0	82	25	6
Canada	2	0	1	45	33	4
Romania	1	0	2	31	64	2
Fiji	0	0	3	27	63	0

QUARTER-FINALS

England	19-10	France
Scotland	28-6	Western Samoa
Australia	19-18	Ireland
New Zealand	29-13	Canada

SEMI-FINALS

England	9-6	Scotland
Australia	16-6	New Zealand

BRONZE FINAL

New Zealand   13-6   Scotland

THE FINAL

Australia   12-6   England

AUSTRALIA	ENGLAND
T: Daly	
C: Lynagh	
P: Lynagh (2)	Webb (2)

LEADING POINTS SCORERS

1. 68   Ralph Keyes (IRE)
2. 66   Michael Lynagh (AUS)
3. 61   Gaving Hastings (SCO)

LEADING TRY SCORERS

1. 6   David Campese (AUS)
= 6   Jean-Baptiste Lafond (FRA)
3. 4   Tim Horan (AUS)
= 4   Brian Robinson (IRE)
= 4   Iwan Tukalo (SCO)
= 4   Rory Underwood (ENG)

Ireland thought they had booked a place in the final four when flanker Gordon Hamilton scored in the 73rd minute, but a try from Wallabies fly-half Michael Lynagh in the dying moments swung the match 19-18 in his side's favour.

Buoyed by that success, Australia went into their semi-final with New Zealand full of confidence. And they put in a memorable performance as they beat the All Blacks 16-6 to administer that side's first-ever Rugby World Cup defeat.

In the other semi-final it was another encounter between historic rivals as England took on Scotland. It turned into a battle of the boot, with Rob Andrew's drop goal giving England a narrow 9-6 win.

Right: Rugby World Cup 1991 proved to be a tournament of shocks as emerging rugby nations, such as Western Samoa against Wales, showed their talent.

There was more pain for Scotland just a few days later as New Zealand beat them in the bronze final, before all eyes turned to Twickenham for England and Australia's showdown.

With a home crowd behind them England were dreaming of glory, but the goal-kicking of Lynagh and a try from Tony Daly secured a 12-6 victory for Australia and their first Rugby World Cup.

RUGBY WORLD CUP 1995
South Africa

After being readmitted to international rugby in 1992, South Africa made their tournament debut as hosts. It proved to be a Rugby World Cup like no other, the Springboks going all the way, carried forward by a wave of emotion that drove them on and united the entire country.

All eyes were on South Africa when they kicked off their Rugby World Cup story as hosts. After an opening-day 27-18 victory over reigning champions Australia, confidence grew and they went on to top Pool A, claiming two more wins over Canada and Romania.

Australia ended up taking the second spot and the beaten finalists from the last tournament, England, joined them in the quarter-finals. Led by the boot of Rob Andrew, England topped Pool B as Western Samoa claimed second place thanks to victories over Argentina and Italy.

In Pool C, waves were being made by the arrival of New Zealand wing Jonah Lomu, who was proving a handful for defenders. Blessed with unbelievable pace and power, he helped the All Blacks top the pool ahead of Ireland, with Wales third and Japan fourth – and they scored a staggering 222 points in the process.

France and Scotland joined them in the knockout stages after they progressed out of Pool D. Both sides defeated Ivory Coast and Tonga, but the French overcame Scotland 22-19 in the final round of matches to go through as pool winners.

France's reward for that was a showdown with Ireland, overcoming them 36-12, thanks largely to the precision kicking of Thierry Lacroix. Waiting for them in the semi-finals would be either Western Samoa or South Africa, who were growing into the tournament with each match.

Western Samoa were beaten as the Springboks claimed an impressive 42-14 win.

On the other side of the draw, Lomu and his New Zealand team-mates showed no sign of slowing down – no matter what their opponents tried. Indeed they ran in six tries to see off Scotland 48-30 and set up a showdown with the winner of England and Australia.

After being denied glory in their own backyard four years earlier, England wanted revenge, and they duly got it as fly-half Andrew nailed a 45-metre drop goal deep into injury time to secure a 25-22 victory.

England's task was now to try and find a way to stop free-scoring New Zealand, and in particular Lomu. He had been unplayable so far, and that proved to be the case in the semi-final. The 20-year-old proved to be unstoppable as he bulldozed his way to four tries in New Zealand's 45-29

RUGBY WORLD CUP
HEROES

JOEL STRANSKY (South Africa)

It may have been captain Francois Pienaar who unified the nation and team at Rugby World Cup 1995, but it was Joel Stransky who kicked them to glory. The fly-half was rock solid with his boot throughout the tournament, particularly in the final. It was then, against New Zealand, that he scored all the Springboks' points, including a drop goal in the second period of extra-time that turned out to be the winning kick.

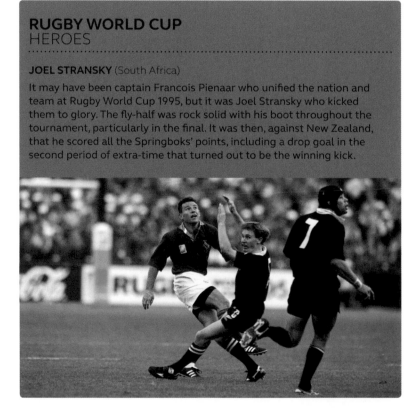

victory in Cape Town.

Their opponents in the final would be South Africa, who had booked their place thanks to Ruben Kruger's solitary try in a 19-15 win over France.

It was expected that New Zealand would continue their rich try-scoring form from earlier on in the tournament, but instead the match was a cagey affair.

South Africa fly-half Joel Stransky and his opposite number, Andrew Mehrtens, kicked nine points each to send the match into extra-time. They once again traded kicks to take the score to 12-12 going into the second period of extra-time.

And it was then that Stransky stepped up to kick the winning drop goal and send the whole of South Africa into celebration.

President Nelson Mandela, famously wearing a Springbok jersey, then presented the Webb Ellis Cup to captain Francois Pienaar – a moment demonstrating that the nation had been united by sport.

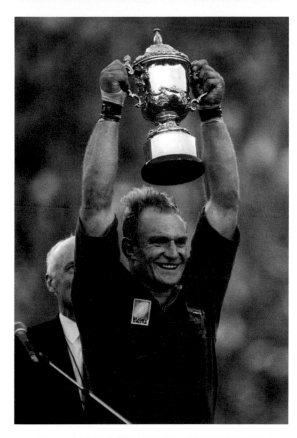

Left: Francois Pienaar holds the Webb Ellis Cup aloft after captaining South Africa to glory.

TOURNAMENT STATISTICS

Host nation: South Africa
Dates: 25 May-24 June, 1995
Teams: 16 (52 during qualifying)
Matches: 32
Overall attendance: 936,900

POOL A	W	D	L	PF	PA	Pts
South Africa	3	0	0	68	26	6
Australia	2	0	1	87	41	4
Canada	1	0	2	45	50	2
Romania	0	0	3	14	97	0

POOL B	W	D	L	PF	PA	Pts
England	3	0	0	95	60	6
Western Samoa	2	0	1	96	88	4
Italy	1	0	2	69	94	2
Argentina	0	0	3	69	87	0

POOL C	W	D	L	PF	PA	Pts
New Zealand	3	0	0	222	45	6
Ireland	2	0	1	93	94	4
Wales	1	0	2	89	68	2
Japan	0	0	3	55	252	0

POOL D	W	D	L	PF	PA	Pts
France	3	0	0	114	47	6
Scotland	2	0	1	149	27	4
Tonga	1	0	2	44	90	2
Ivory Coast	0	0	3	29	172	0

QUARTER-FINALS

France	36-12	Ireland
South Africa	42-14	Western Samoa
England	25-22	Australia
New Zealand	48-30	Scotland

SEMI-FINALS

South Africa	19-15	France
New Zealand	45-29	England

BRONZE FINAL

France	19-9	England

THE FINAL

South Africa   15-12   New Zealand
              (aet)

	SOUTH AFRICA	NEW ZEALAND
P:	Stransky (3)	Mehrtens (3)
DG:	Stransky (2)	Mehrtens

LEADING POINTS SCORERS
1. 112   Thierry Lacroix (FRA)
2. 104   Gavin Hastings (SCO)
3. 84   Andrew Mehrtens (NZL)

LEADING TRY SCORERS
1. 7   Marc Ellis (NZL)
= 7   Jonah Lomu (NZL)
3. 5   Gavin Hastings (SCO)
= 5   Rory Underwood (ENG)

RUGBY WORLD CUP 1999
Wales

Wales, and the brand new Millennium Stadium in Cardiff, were the hosts of the first Rugby World Cup staged during the game's professional era. Matches also took place in England, France, Ireland and Scotland as 20 teams came together for a tournament that finished with Australia becoming champions for the second time.

With 20 teams taking part in Rugby World Cup 1999, the tournament took on a new format. Five pools of four were drawn, with the top team from each one guaranteed a place in the quarter-finals.

The five runners-up and the best third-placed team then competed in play-off matches to complete the line-up for the quarter-finals.

The southern hemisphere nations were in fine form from the start and Australia, New Zealand and South Africa all topped their pools with 100 per cent records.

France achieved the same feat and hosts Wales progressed as winners too after finishing ahead of Argentina and Samoa on points difference.

England, Fiji, Ireland and Scotland joined Argentina and Samoa in the new look quarter-final play-offs as they all tried to keep their Rugby World Cup dreams alive.

Led by the boot of Jonny Wilkinson, England toppled Fiji 45-24, and they were joined by Scotland who defeated Samoa 35-20. Ireland, however, missed out on the quarter-finals for the first time as Argentina stunned them 28-24 in Lens.

Argentina's run ended in the last eight, as they lost to France, who showed that they were contenders to go all the way. The French ran in five tries in a 47-26 win, but they were the only northern hemisphere team to make the semi-finals.

Australia saw off hosts Wales 24-9 in Cardiff thanks to two tries by scrum-half George Gregan, while New Zealand defeated Scotland 30-18 in Edinburgh. England fell too as Clive Woodward, coaching at his first Rugby World Cup, saw his team undone by the boot of South Africa fly-half Jannie de Beer – who scored 35 points to help the Springboks win 44-21.

De Beer carried his fine form into the semi-finals for South Africa's encounter with Australia at Twickenham. Both he and Wallabies full-back Matt Burke kicked 18 points to send the match into extra-time.

The duo traded scores with the boot again, before Australia fly-half Stephen Larkham landed a crucial drop goal to make it 24-21. Burke then slotted a penalty to secure the win and send the Wallabies into the final once again.

TOURNAMENT STATISTICS

Host nation: Wales
Dates: 1 October-6 November, 1999
Teams: 20 (71 during qualifying)
Matches: 41
Overall attendance: 1,556,572

POOL A	W	D	L	PF	PA	Pts
South Africa	3	0	0	132	35	6
Scotland	2	0	1	120	58	4
Uruguay	1	0	2	42	97	2
Spain	0	0	3	81	22	0

POOL B	W	D	L	PF	PA	Pts
New Zealand	3	0	0	176	28	6
England	2	0	1	184	47	4
Tonga	1	0	2	47	171	2
Italy	0	0,	3	35	196	0

POOL C	W	D	L	PF	PA	Pts
France	3	0	0	108	52	6
Fiji	2	0	1	124	68	4
Canada	1	0	2	114	82	2
Namibia	0	0	3	42	186	0

POOL D	W	D	L	PF	PA	Pts
Wales	2	0	1	118	71	4
Samoa	2	0	1	97	72	4
Argentina	2	0	1	83	51	4
Japan	0	0	3	36	40	0

POOL E	W	D	L	PF	PA	Pts
Australia	3	0	0	135	31	6
Ireland	2	0	1	100	45	4
Romania	1	0	2	50	126	2
USA	0	0	3	52	135	0

QUARTER-FINAL PLAY-OFFS

England	45-24	Fiji
Scotland	35-20	Samoa
Argentina	28-24	Ireland

QUARTER-FINALS

Australia	24-9	Wales
South Africa	44-21	England
New Zealand	30-18	Scotland
France	47-26	Argentina

SEMI-FINALS

Australia	27-21	South Africa
	(aet)	
France	43-31	New Zealand

BRONZE FINAL

South Africa 22-18 New Zealand

THE FINAL

Australia 35-12 France

AUSTRALIA	FRANCE
T: Tune, Finegan	
C: Burke (2)	
P: Burke (7)	Lamaison (4)

LEADING POINTS SCORERS

1. 102 Gonzalo Quesada (ARG)
2. 101 Matt Burke (AUS)
3. 97 Jannie de Beer (RSA)

LEADING TRY SCORERS

1. 8 Jonah Lomu (NZL)
2. 6 Jeff Wilson (NZL)
3. 4 Keith Wood (IRE)
= 4 Philippe Bernat-Salles (FRA)
= 4 Viliame Satala (FIJ)
= 4 Dan Luger (ENG)

The other semi-final proved to be just as dramatic when France pulled off an amazing comeback to beat New Zealand. The All Blacks were hot favourites for the match, largely due to the presence of wing Jonah Lomu – who duly scored twice. However, their 24-10 lead was overhauled by a resurgent France, who scored 33 points in as many minutes to claim an incredible 43-31 victory.

Les Bleus now went into the final believing they could win their first Rugby World Cup. Australia stood in their way, desperate to lift the Webb Ellis Cup again after doing so in 1991.

In the end, it was the Wallabies who were the ones celebrating after Burke kicked 25 points during a 35-12 victory.

Captain John Eales was duly presented with the Webb Ellis Cup by Her Majesty The Queen and once again Australia were crowned champions of the world.

Left: Captain John Eales holds aloft the Webb Ellis Cup as Australia are crowned world champions again.

RUGBY WORLD CUP 2003
Australia

England travelled to Rugby World Cup 2003 as favourites after developing into a formidable side under coach Clive Woodward since the last tournament. Led by captain Martin Johnson and the deadly kicking of fly-half Jonny Wilkinson, they managed to go all the way in Australia to become the northern hemisphere's first world champions.

After Sydney had hosted a hugely successful Olympic Games in 2000, there was a buzz in Australia as Rugby World Cup 2003 was staged across the country.

The hosts were determined to be victorious once again after winning the tournament in 1999 in Wales. The Wallabies started in ominous style, topping Pool A with four wins from four, including against Argentina and Ireland. They also ran in 22 tries in the 142-0 win over Namibia, in a clear demonstration of their attacking talent.

Like Australia, England made a perfect start to the tournament, winning all their matches in Pool C. A 25-6 victory over South Africa, during which Jonny Wilkinson kicked 20 points, proved decisive, enabling them to claim top spot after both sides had recorded wins over Georgia, Uruguay and Samoa to reach the quarter-finals.

Elsewhere, France were looking dangerous too, racing through as winners of Pool B. Les Bleus achieved a 100 per cent record in their opening four matches, which included a 51-9 victory over pool runners-up Scotland.

New Zealand and Wales completed the quarter-final line-up after both made it out of Pool D.

In line with expectations, the All Blacks emerged as pool winners after scoring 282 points in their four victories. Their match with Wales for top spot proved to be a Rugby World Cup classic: the teams scored 12 tries in an encounter that New Zealand edged 53-37.

Awaiting the All Blacks in the quarter-finals were South Africa, and the two went head to head in Melbourne. In the end, New Zealand had too much for the Springboks and 16 points from Leon MacDonald guided them through 29-9.

Another heavyweight encounter in the quarter-finals was England's match with rivals Wales. After negotiating the pool stages, the pressure was on Clive Woodward's side to kick on, and they were given an almighty scare in Brisbane. Wales led at half-time, thanks to tries from Stephen Jones and Colin Charvis, but England replied through Will Greenwood and the boot of Wilkinson to progress 28-17.

RUGBY WORLD CUP
HEROES

MARTIN JOHNSON (England)

If anyone personified the spirit of the England team that went all the way in 2003, it was Martin Johnson. Fly-half Jonny Wilkinson may have grabbed the headlines for his last-minute drop-goal, but Johnson was the glue that held the team together. A brilliant captain who gave his all for the shirt, he led from the front and was crucial at the set-piece too. One of the greatest captains of all time.

On the other side of the draw, Australia were also thankful to their goal-kicker as Elton Flatley scored 18 points during their 33-16 win over Scotland.

France's Frédéric Michalak was finding his groove too and his haul of 23 points ensured Les Bleus overcame Ireland 43-21 in Melbourne. This set up a showdown with England in the semi-finals, where the two sides battled it out in the driving rain in Sydney. In the horrible conditions, it was left to Wilkinson to kick his team through – and he duly did by scoring all of his side's points in a 24-7 victory.

England's opponents in the final were Australia, who had put in an inspired display against New Zealand in the semi-finals to beat them 22-10. The final turned into a battle of the boot and once again Wilkinson was the hero, scoring the decisive drop goal with seconds to spare in extra-time.

Above: England became the first northern hemisphere Rugby World Cup winners in 2003.

TOURNAMENT STATISTICS

Host nation: Australia
Dates: 10 October-22 November, 2003
Teams: 20 (89 during qualifying)
Matches: 48
Overall attendance: 1,837,547

POOL A	W	D	L	PF	PA	Pts
Australia	4	0	0	273	32	18
Ireland	3	0	1	141	56	15
Argentina	2	0	2	140	57	11
Romania	1	0	3	65	192	5
Namibia	0	0	4	28	310	0

POOL B	W	D	L	PF	PA	Pts
France	4	0	0	204	70	20
Scotland	3	0	1	102	97	14
Fiji	2	0	2	98	114	10
USA	1	0	3	86	125	6
Japan	0	0	4	79	163	0

POOL C	W	D	L	PF	PA	Pts
England	4	0	0	255	47	19
South Africa	3	0	1	184	60	15
Samoa	2	0	2	138	117	10
Uruguay	1	0	3	56	255	4
Georgia	0	0	4	46	200	0

POOL D	W	D	L	PF	PA	Pts
New Zealand	4	0	0	282	57	20
Wales	3	0	1	132	98	14
Italy	2	0	2	77	123	8
Canada	1	0	3	54	135	5
Tonga	0	0	4	46	178	1

QUARTER-FINALS

New Zealand	29-9	South Africa
Australia	33-16	Scotland
France	43-21	Ireland
England	28-17	Wales

SEMI-FINALS

Australia	22-10	New Zealand
England	24-7	France

BRONZE FINAL

New Zealand	40-13	France

THE FINAL

England	20-17	Australia
	(aet)	

ENGLAND		AUSTRALIA
T:	Robinson	Tuqiri
P:	Wilkinson (4)	Flatley (4)
DG:	Wilkinson	

LEADING POINTS SCORERS

1. 113 Jonny Wilkinson (ENG)
2. 103 Frédéric Michalak (FRA)
3. 100 Elton Flatley (AUS)

LEADING TRY SCORERS

1. 7 Doug Howlett (NZL)
= 7 Mils Muliaina (NZL)
3. 6 Joe Rokocoko (NZL)

RUGBY WORLD CUP 2007
France

More than two million fans packed out stadia in France as Rugby World Cup fever swept the nation. The tournament proved to be one of the most dramatic in history: Argentina defied the odds to finish third and South Africa were crowned world champions for the second time in their history.

As hosts of Rugby World Cup 2007, the pressure was on France to succeed and potentially even lift the Webb Ellis Cup for the first time. However, they kicked off the tournament in the worst way possible, being stunned by Argentina in Paris 17-12.

Los Pumas put in an incredible performance full of grit and determination, and they were worthy winners of a match that would set the tone for the whole competition.

Argentina went on to win all of their matches in Pool D to go through in top spot, meaning that France had to settle for second place.

It was a similar story for reigning champions England, who finished runners-up in Pool A. England, now coached by Brian Ashton, suffered a 36-0 loss to pool winners South Africa, which suggested the team would struggle to recreate the heroics from four years earlier.

England's fellow finalists from Rugby World Cup 2003, Australia, enjoyed a better start, scoring more than 200 points as they finished top of Pool B. The Wallabies had expected to be joined by Wales in the quarter-finals, but instead they were on the plane home after losing 38-34 to runners-up Fiji.

Elsewhere in Pool C, New Zealand cruised through to the knockout stages with a perfect record and 309 points. They were joined in the quarter-finals by Scotland, who qualified in second place, and their reward was a showdown with surprise package Argentina.

The South Americans put in another brilliant display to secure a 19-13 victory in Paris. Argentina's run to the semi-finals was proving to be one of the stories of the tournament, and then came another result that sent similar shockwaves through the rugby world: New Zealand were knocked out by France.

The All Blacks had never failed to make the last four of a Rugby World Cup, but tries from Thierry Dusautoir and Yannick Jauzion ended that run as France won 20-18.

After a shaky start to the tournament, England were starting to recover and a magnificent performance from the scrum helped them overcome Australia 12-10 in Marseille.

South Africa joined them in the semi-finals with a 37-20 win over Fiji, which set up a meeting with surprise package Argentina. The match proved a step too far for Los Pumas, who lost 37-13, but they had won fans all over the world with their performances.

In the other semi-final, England's

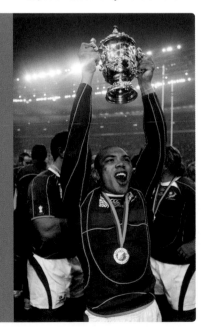

resurgence continued as they toppled hosts France in Paris. Wing Josh Lewsey scored after two minutes and the reliable boot of Wilkinson added nine points to secure a 14-9 victory that set up a rematch with South Africa.

In the pool stages, the Springboks had been comfortable winners, but the final proved to be a much cagier affair. Neither side was able to score a try, although England wing Mark Cueto was inches from doing so, only for his foot to go into touch.

Instead, it came down to a battle of the boot and South Africa held their nerve to win rugby's greatest prize.

Right: Argentina stunned the rugby world in 2007 by making it all the way to the Rugby World Cup semi-finals.

TOURNAMENT STATISTICS

Host nation: France
Dates: 7 September–20 October, 2007
Teams: 20 (94 during qualifying)
Matches: 48
Overall attendance: 2,245,731

POOL A	W	D	L	PF	PA	Pts
South Africa	4	0	0	189	47	19
England	3	0	1	108	88	14
Tonga	2	0	2	89	96	9
Samoa	1	0	3	69	143	5
USA	0	0	4	61	142	1

POOL B	W	D	L	PF	PA	Pts
Australia	4	0	0	215	41	20
Fiji	3	0	1	114	136	15
Wales	2	0	2	168	105	12
Japan	0	1	3	64	210	3
Canada	0	1	3	51	210	2

POOL C	W	D	L	PF	PA	Pts
New Zealand	4	0	0	309	35	20
Scotland	3	0	1	116	66	14
Italy	2	0	2	85	117	9
Romania	1	0	3	40	161	5
Portugal	0	0	4	38	209	1

POOL D	W	D	L	PF	PA	Pts
Argentina	4	0	0	143	33	18
France	3	0	1	188	37	15
Ireland	2	0	2	64	82	9
Georgia	1	0	3	50	111	5
Namibia	0	0	4	30	212	0

QUARTER-FINALS

England	12-10	Australia
France	20-18	New Zealand
South Africa	37-20	Fiji
Argentina	19-13	Scotland

SEMI-FINALS

England	14-9	France
South Africa	37-13	Argentina

BRONZE FINAL

Argentina	34-10	France

THE FINAL

South Africa	15-6	England

SOUTH AFRICA	ENGLAND
P: Steyn,	Wilkinson (2)
Montgomery (4)	

LEADING POINTS SCORERS

1. 105 Percy Montgomery (RSA)
2. 91 Felipe Contepomi (ARG)
3. 67 Jonny Wilkinson (ENG)

LEADING TRY SCORERS

1. 8 Bryan Habana (RSA)
2. 7 Drew Mitchell (AUS)
3. 6 Doug Howlett (NZL)
= 6 Shane Williams (WAL)

RUGBY WORLD CUP 2011
New Zealand

Not since the inaugural Rugby World Cup in 1987 had New Zealand hosted or won the tournament. So expectations were high as they stepped up to stage the competition in 2011. The All Blacks duly delivered, narrowly beating France in the final to end 24 years of hurt.

After years of near misses, the pressure was very much on New Zealand to go all the way at Rugby World Cup 2011. The All Blacks started in formidable fashion, winning their first three Pool A matches, against Tonga, Japan and France.

Ahead of their final pool match, against Canada, however, disaster struck as star fly-half Dan Carter suffered a groin injury that kept him out for the rest of the tournament. New Zealand went on to win the match, but filling his position would be a continued problem.

Reigning champions South Africa also enjoyed a perfect start as they progressed as Pool D winners, with Wales joining them in the quarter-finals after a key win over Samoa.

Argentina, the surprise package from Rugby World Cup 2007, again reached the knockout stages – but this time they had to settle for second place as England topped Pool B.

Ireland and Australia completed the quarter-final line-up by making it out of Pool C. The Irish recorded four wins to finish top, including an impressive 15-6 victory over Australia.

All eyes turned towards the All Blacks, who would have to cope without Carter, as knockout rugby returned. Colin Slade, who had come in for the Canada match, started the quarter-final against Argentina but he too was struck down by injury.

Scrum-half Piri Weepu slotted in at fly-half for the rest of the match and kicked seven penalties as New Zealand secured a 33-10 victory.

Waiting for the All Blacks in the semi-finals would be Australia after they knocked out defending champions South Africa in a tight match in Wellington.

On the other side of the draw, there were two northern hemisphere meetings, and it was Ireland and England who were sent home. Wales ran in three tries to beat Ireland 22-10, while France got revenge on their semi-final defeat to England four years before by winning 19-12.

Les Bleus then booked a spot in the final courtesy of a 9-8 victory over Wales, in which captain Sam Warburton was dismissed inside 20 minutes. It left the Welsh playing with 14 men for more than an hour and, despite an heroic effort, it proved a bridge too far.

New Zealand clicked into gear: despite fielding their third-choice fly-half, Aaron Cruden, they booked a place in the final with a 20-6 win over Australia, with Ma'a Nonu scoring a try and Weepu adding four penalties.

Now it was all about finishing the job in front of a packed Eden Park, but again disaster struck and Cruden limped off just before half-time.

RUGBY WORLD CUP
HEROES

Richie McCaw (New Zealand)
After suffering heartbreak at Rugby World Cup 2007, Richie McCaw was determined to make amends. A foot injury dogged the flanker throughout the tournament, but he was still able to lead his team to glory with some incredible performances at the breakdown. There was no doubting the commitment of one of New Zealand's greatest ever players, summed up by coach Graham Henry after the final: "He can hardly walk and how he played today I just don't know."

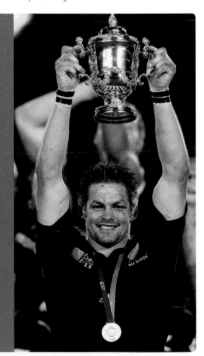

TOURNAMENT STATISTICS

Host nations: New Zealand
Dates: 9 September-23 October, 2011
Teams: 20 (91 during qualifying)
Matches: 48
Overall attendance: 1,477,294

POOL A	W	D	L	PF	PA	Pts
New Zealand	4	0	0	240	49	20
France	2	0	2	124	96	11
Tonga	2	0	2	80	98	9
Canada	1	1	2	82	168	6
Japan	0	1	3	60	104	2

POOL B	W	D	L	PF	PA	Pts
England	4	0	0	137	34	18
Argentina	3	0	1	90	40	14
Scotland	2	0	2	73	59	11
Georgia	1	0	3	48	90	4
Romania	0	0	4	44	169	0

POOL C	W	D	L	PF	PA	Pts
Ireland	4	0	0	135	34	17
Australia	3	0	1	173	48	15
Italy	2	0	2	92	95	10
USA	1	0	3	38	122	4
Russia	0	0	4	57	196	1

POOL D	W	D	L	PF	PA	Pts
South Africa	4	0	0	166	24	18
Wales	3	0	1	180	34	15
Samoa	2	0	2	91	49	10
Fiji	1	0	3	59	167	5
Namibia	0	0	4	44	266	0

QUARTER-FINALS

Wales	22-10	Ireland
France	19-12	England
Australia	11-9	South Africa
New Zealand	33-10	Argentina

SEMI-FINALS

France	9-8	Wales
New Zealand	20-6	Australia

BRONZE FINAL

Australia	21-18	Wales

THE FINAL

New Zealand	8-7	France

NEW ZEALAND	FRANCE
T: Woodcock	Dusautoir
C:	Trinh-Duc
P: Donald	

LEADING POINTS SCORERS

1. 62 Morné Steyn (RSA)
2. 52 James O'Connor (AUS)
3. 45 Kurt Morath (TGA)

LEADING TRY SCORERS

1. 6 Chris Ashton (ENG)
= 6 Vincent Clerc (FRA)
3. 5 Adam Ashley-Cooper (AUS)
= 5 Keith Earls (IRE)
= 5 Israel Dagg (NZL)

The injury curse of the fly-half had returned. Replacing him was Stephen Donald, the emergency call-up who had been on holiday just weeks earlier, fishing; in fact he had watched the opening ceremony sitting on a beach in Otago. He came on and kicked what turned out to be the winning penalty in the 46th minute, making it 8-0.

France hit back with a try from captain Thierry Dusautoir, converted by François Trinh-Duc, himself a first-half replacement for the injured fly-half Morgan Parra, but it was not enough. Les Bleus threw everything they had at the All Blacks, but Richie McCaw's men held their discipline, limiting Trinh-Duc to a solitary – missed – long-range penalty attempt with 15 minutes remaining. The wait was over: New Zealand were champions again.

Left: Stephen Donald began Rugby World Cup 2011 on a fishing holiday in Otago; he finished it kicking the All Blacks to glory.

RUGBY WORLD CUP 2015
England

After the success of Rugby World Cup 2011 in New Zealand, it was the northern hemisphere's turn to stage the tournament, with England as hosts. It proved to be a memorable competition, with plenty of shocks along the way. In the end, New Zealand became the first team to retain the Webb Ellis Cup.

All eyes were on England as hosts of Rugby World Cup 2015, and there was intense pressure on them to succeed.

They started in a steady fashion, defeating Fiji 35-11 at Twickenham, but from there it began to unravel for coach Stuart Lancaster and his side. England faced Wales next and, leading 22-12 with 30 minutes to play, victory looked assured. However, the Welsh staged a brilliant comeback, stunning England 28-25, with fly-half Dan Biggar scoring 23 points.

Just days later it got even worse

for the hosts: they were beaten by an electric Australia, who scored three tries during a deserved 33-13 win.

After three matches, England were out and, for the first time, the Rugby World Cup main hosts had failed to get out of their pool.

The drama was not reserved to Pool A, though. In Pool B, Japan pulled off one of the greatest shocks in the sport's history: Eddie Jones' team defeated South Africa 34-32 in Brighton, with a last-minute try from Karne Hesketh sending the two-time

champions to an opening-game loss.

The Springboks duly recovered to finish in top spot with Japan, who claimed two more wins, unluckily beaten to a quarter-final berth by Scotland, courtesy of two bonus points.

On the other side of the draw, events went more according to plan as New Zealand and Argentina finished first and second respectively in Pool C. In Pool D, Ireland won their four matches to finish ahead of France.

Les Bleus' prize was a rematch in the quarter-finals with their conquerors from four years earlier, New Zealand. This time, however, the match was not close, the All Blacks scoring nine tries on their way to a 62-13 victory.

It turned out to be a clean sweep for the southern hemisphere in the quarter-finals, as all four of them progressed.

South Africa defeated Wales 23-19 thanks to scrum-half Fourie du Preez's 75th-minute try, while Argentina put in one of the performances of the tournament to beat Ireland 43-20.

Australia completed the set by defeating Scotland 35-34, with fly-half Bernard Foley's penalty in the dying moments providing the cruellest of knockout blows.

This meant that for the first time in history there was no northern hemisphere representation in the Rugby World Cup semi-finals.

After squeezing through against Scotland, Australia went up a gear

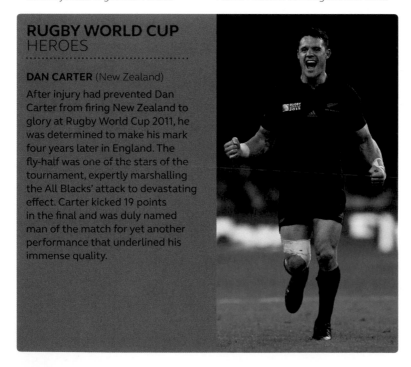

RUGBY WORLD CUP
HEROES
....

DAN CARTER (New Zealand)
After injury had prevented Dan Carter from firing New Zealand to glory at Rugby World Cup 2011, he was determined to make his mark four years later in England. The fly-half was one of the stars of the tournament, expertly marshalling the All Blacks' attack to devastating effect. Carter kicked 19 points in the final and was duly named man of the match for yet another performance that underlined his immense quality.

against Argentina to earn a spot in the final. Adam Ashley-Cooper, the Wallabies' "Mr Versatile", was the star of the match, his hat-trick of tries securing a 29-15 victory.

Waiting for them in the final were the reigning champions, New Zealand, who had overturned a five-point deficit at half-time in their semi-final to overcome South Africa 20-18.

Now the All Blacks were looking to make history by becoming the first team to retain the Rugby World Cup. Tries from Nehe Milner-Skudder and Ma'a Nonu saw them race into a 21-3 lead. Australia clawed it back to 21-17, but Beauden Barrett's try, and Carter's 19 points, made the final score 34-17.

Once again, Richie McCaw and the All Blacks had their hands on the Webb Ellis Cup.

Right: England's tournament was over after three matches as the hosts went out.

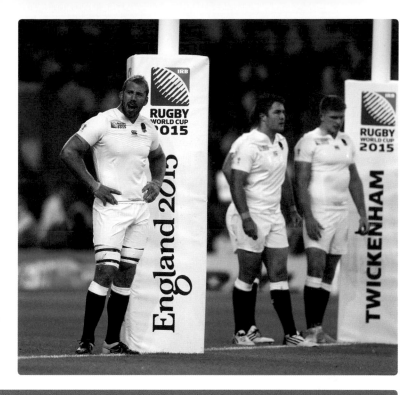

TOURNAMENT STATISTICS

Host nation: England
Dates: 18 September-31 October, 2015
Teams: 20 (96 during qualifying)
Matches: 48
Overall attendance: 2,477,805

POOL A	W	D	L	PF	PA	Pts
Australia	4	0	0	141	35	17
Wales	3	0	1	111	62	13
England	2	0	2	133	75	11
Fiji	1	0	3	84	101	5
Uruguay	0	0	4	30	226	0

POOL B	W	D	L	PF	PA	Pts
South Africa	3	0	1	176	56	16
Scotland	3	0	1	136	93	14
Japan	3	0	1	98	100	12
Samoa	1	0	3	69	124	6
USA	0	0	4	50	156	0

POOL C	W	D	L	PF	PA	Pts
New Zealand	4	0	0	174	49	19
Argentina	3	0	1	179	70	15
Georgia	2	0	2	53	123	8
Tonga	1	0	3	70	130	6
Namibia	0	0	4	70	174	1

POOL D	W	D	L	PF	PA	Pts
Ireland	4	0	0	134	35	18
France	3	0	1	120	63	14
Italy	2	0	2	74	88	10
Romania	1	0	3	60	129	4
Canada	0	0	4	58	131	2

QUARTER-FINALS
South Africa   23-19   Wales
New Zealand   62-13   France
Ireland   20-43   Argentina
Australia   35-34   Scotland

SEMI-FINALS
South Africa   18-20   New Zealand
Argentina   15-29   Australia

BRONZE FINAL
South Africa   24-13   Argentina

THE FINAL
New Zealand   34-17   Australia

NEW ZEALAND		AUSTRALIA
T:	Milner-Skudder, Nonu, Barrett	Pocock, Kuridrani
C:	Carter (2)	Foley (2)
P:	Carter (4)	Foley
DG:	Carter	

LEADING POINTS SCORERS
1.   97   Nicolás Sánchez (ARG)
2.   93   Handré Pollard (RSA)
3.   82   Bernard Foley (AUS)
=   82   Dan Carter (NZL)

LEADING TRY SCORERS
1.   8   Julian Savea (NZL)
2.   6   Nehe Milner-Skudder (NZL)
3.   5   Bryan Habana (RSA)
=   5   Gareth Davis (WAL)
=   5   Juan Imhoff (ARG)
=   5   JP Pietersen (RSA)

JAPAN'S BRAVE BLOSSOMS BLOOM TO SNARE SPRINGBOKS

19 September, 2015: Brighton Community Stadium, Brighton

Prior to their meeting with South Africa at Rugby World Cup 2015, Japan had not won a match in the tournament since 1991. It meant that they headed to Brighton for their encounter with the two-time champions hoping to pull off one of the game's greatest shocks. At half-time, they were trailing South Africa 12-10, and such a result looked unlikely. Japan refused to fold, though, and the steady goal kicking of full-back Ayumu Goromaru, who finished with 24 points, kept them in the match. The two sides continued to exchange scores and, as the match ticked into added time, it was South Africa who led 32-29. It looked as though the Springboks would hold on, but in the 84th minute Japan wing Karne Hesketh scored in the corner to the delight of the Brighton crowd.

Right: Fans and Japan players go wild after they scored a last-minute try to beat South Africa in 2015.

![Rugby World Cup Japan 2019 logo]

**RUGBY
WORLD CUP™**
JAPAN日本 2019

RUGBY WORLD CUP
FACTS &
STATS

Winning the Rugby World Cup is the ultimate prize for any player. However, by taking part in the game's greatest event, players have the chance to write their name into the history books with a one-off performance or a career spanning several tournaments. From the biggest margin of victory to the youngest try-scorer, they are all packed into this section of Rugby World Cup trivia, and the stars of 2019 will be trying to join them.

Left: Bryan Habana shares the overall record with Jonah Lomu for the most tries – 15 – in Rugby World Cup history.

RUGBY WORLD CUP FACTS & STATS: TEAMS

TEAM RECORDS

Biggest victories:
(Position, margin, winner v opponent, venue, date, score)
1. 142 Australia v Namibia, Adelaide, 25 Oct, 2003, 142-0
2. 128 New Zealand v Japan, Bloemfontein, 4 Jun, 1995, 145-17
3. 98 New Zealand v Italy, Huddersfield, 14 Oct, 1999, 101-3
= 98 England v Uruguay, Brisbane, 2 Nov, 2003, 111-13
5. 95 New Zealand v Portugal, Lyon, 15 Sep, 2007, 108-13

Most matches played:
50 New Zealand

Most wins:
44 New Zealand

Most defeats:
22 Japan, Romania and USA

Fewest wins:
0 Ivory Coast, Namibia, Portugal, Russia, Spain and Zimbabwe

Most matches without a win:
19 Namibia, 1999–2015

Most tries:
311 New Zealand

Most points:
2,302 New Zealand

Most drop goals:
21 England

Most penalties kicked:
135 France

Most conversions:
226 New Zealand

Most tries in a match:
22 Australia v Namibia , Adelaide, 25 Oct, 2003

Most points by one team in a match:
145 New Zealand v Japan, Bloemfontein, 4 Jun, 1995

Most points by both teams in a match:
162 New Zealand v Japan (145-17), Bloemfontein, 4 Jun, 1995

Most tries in a tournament:
52 New Zealand in 2003

Most points in a tournament:
361 New Zealand in 2003

Fewest points in a tournament:
14 Romania in 1995

Only team to have played at a Rugby World Cup and not scored a try:
Spain

Most points scored in a losing cause:
37 Wales v New Zealand (53-37), Pool D, Sydney, 2 Nov, 2003

Most tries scored in a losing cause:
5 Wales v Fiji (38-34), Nantes, 29 Sep, 2007

Teams failing to score a single point:
(Score, team v opponent, venue, date)
0-89 Ivory Coast v Scotland, Rustenberg, 26 May, 1995
0-20 Canada v South Africa, Port Elizabeth, 3 Jun, 1995
0-48 Spain v Scotland, Murrayfield, 16 Oct, 1999
0-142 Namibia v Australia, Adelaide, 25 Oct, 2003
0-36 England v South Africa, Paris, 14 Sep, 2007
0-42 Romania v Scotland, Murrayfield, 18 Sep, 2007
0-40 Scotland v New Zealand, Murrayfield, 23 Sep, 2007
0-30 Namibia v Georgia, Lens, 26 Sep, 2007
0-87 Nambia v South Africa, Auckland, 22 Sep, 2011
0-66 Fiji v Wales, Hamilton, 2 Oct, 2011
0-64 USA v South Africa, Olympic Stadium, 7 Oct, 2015

Matches decided by a single point:
(Score, winner v opponent, venue, date)
22-21 Wales v Australia, Rotorua,
       18 Jun, 1987
19-18 Australia v Ireland, Dublin,
       20 Oct, 1991
24-23 Ireland v Wales, Johannesburg,
       4 Jun, 1995
19-18 Fiji v USA, Brisbane, 15 Oct, 2003
16-15 Ireland v Argentina, Adelaide,
       26 Oct, 2003
17-16 Australia v Ireland, Melbourne,
       1 Nov, 2003
17-16 South Africa v Wales,
       Wellington, 11 Sep, 2011
13-12 Argentina v Scotland,
       Wellington, 25 Sep, 2011
9-8   France v Wales, Auckland,
       15 Oct, 2011
8-7   New Zealand v France,
       Auckland, 23 Oct, 2011
17-16 Georgia v Namibia, Exeter, 7 Oct,
       2015
35-34 Australia v Scotland,
       Twickenham, 18 Oct, 2015

DISCIPLINE

Number of red cards:
3 Canada and Tonga
2 Samoa, South Africa and Wales
1 Argentina, Australia, Fiji, Namibia
   and Uruguay

First red card at Rugby World Cup:
Huw Richards (WAL) against New
Zealand in the 1987 semi-final

Most red cards in a match:
3 South Africa (John Dalton) against
   Canada (Gareth Rees and Rod
   Snow) in Port Elizabeth in 1995

Number of yellow cards:
11 Tonga
10 Argentina
9   Fiji, France, Namibia and New
    Zealand
8   South Africa and USA
7   Australia, Georgia and Romania
6   Italy and Samoa
5   Canada, England, Ireland and
    Scotland
3   Wales
2   Japan and Uruguay

Most yellow cards received by a player:
3 Fabio Ongaro (ITA)

COACHES
Rugby World Cup-winning coaches:
Year, coach (country)
1987   Brian Lochore (NZL)
1991   Bob Dwyer (AUS)
1995   Kitch Christie (RSA)
1999   Rod Macqueen (AUS)
2003   Clive Woodward (ENG)
2007   Jake White (RSA)
2011   Graham Henry (NZL)
2015   Steve Hansen (NZL)

First person to play at a Rugby World Cup before coaching a team at another:
Daniel Dubroca played for France at
the inaugural Rugby World Cup in 1987
and coached them in 1991.

Best performance by a coach in charge of the defending champions:
In 2015 Steve Hansen became the
first coach to successfully guide the
defending champions, in this case
New Zealand, to retaining the Webb
Ellis Cup. Before that the best result
achieved by defending champions had
been to finish runners-up, as Eddie
Jones did with Australia in 2003 and
Brian Ashton with England in 2007.

Worst performance by a coach in charge of the defending champions:
Both Bob Dwyer, in charge of Australia
in 1995, and Peter de Villiers, South
Africa coach in 2011, went out in the
quarter-final of the Rugby World Cup.

Left: England, thanks to 14 from Jonny
Wilkinson, have the most drop goals in
Rugby World Cup history with 21.

Right: New Zealand's Steve Hansen (left, in
2015) was the first man to coach a team to
retain the Webb Ellis Cup.

RUGBY WORLD CUP FACTS & STATS: PLAYERS

TRY-SCORING RECORDS
Most tries:
(Position, tries, player, country, Rugby World Cup span)
1. 15 Bryan Habana, South Africa, 2007-15
= 15 Jonah Lomu, New Zealand, 1995-99
3. 14 Drew Mitchell, Australia, 2007-15
4. 13 Doug Howlett, New Zealand, 2003-07
5. 11 Adam Ashley-Cooper, Australia, 2011-15
= 11 Chris Latham, Australia, 1999-2007
= 11 Josevata Rokocoko, New Zealand, 2003-07
= 11 Rory Underwood, England, 1987-95
= 11 Vincent Clerc, France, 2007-11
10. 10 Brian Lima, Samoa, 2007-11
= 10 David Campese, Australia, 1987-95
= 10 Shane Williams, Wales, 2003-11

Leading try-scorers by tournament:
Year, tries, player (country)

Year	Tries	Player (country)
1987	6	Craig Green (NZL)
		John Kirwan (NZL)
1991	6	David Campese (AUS)
		Jean-Baptiste Lafond (FRA)
1995	7	Marc Ellis (NZL)
		Jonah Lomu (NZL)
1999	8	Jonah Lomu (NZL)
2003	7	Doug Howlett (NZL)
		Mils Muliaina(NZL)
2007	8	Bryan Habana (RSA)
2011	6	Chris Ashton (ENG)
		Vincent Clerc (FRA)
2015	8	Julian Savea (NZL)

Most tries in a match:
6 Marc Ellis (NZL) against Japan in Bloemfontein in 1995

Most tries in a single tournament:
8 Jonah Lomu (NZL) in 1999
Bryan Habana (RSA) in 2007
Julian Savea (NZL) in 2015

First-ever Rugby World Cup try:
A penalty try for New Zealand against Italy in the opening match of the 1987 tournament

Most matches played without scoring a try:
22 Jason Leonard (ENG, 1991-2003)

Youngest try-scorer:
George North (WAL) was 19 years and 166 days old when he scored two tries against Namibia in New Plymouth on 26 September, 2011

Oldest try-scorer:
Diego Ormaechea (URU) was 40 years and 13 days old when he scored against Spain at Galashiels on 2 October, 1999

POINTS-SCORING RECORDS
Most points:
Position, points, player (country, Rugby World Cup span)
1. 277 Jonny Wilkinson (ENG, 1999-2011)
2. 227 Gavin Hastings (SCO, 1987-95)
3. 195 Michael Lynagh (AUS, 1987-95)
4. 191 Daniel Carter (NZL, 2007-15)
5. 170 Grant Fox (NZL, 1987-91)
6. 163 Andrew Mehrtens (NZL, 1995-99)
7. 140 Chris Paterson (SCO, 1999-2011)
8. 136 Frédéric Michalak (FRA, 2003-15)
9. 135 Gonzalo Quesada (ARG, 1999-2003)
10. 125 Matt Burke (AUS, 1995-2003)
= 125 Felipe Contepomi (ARG, 1999-2011)
= 125 Nicky Little (FIJ, 1999-2007)

Most points in a match:
45 Simon Culhane (NZL) against Japan in 1995

Most points in a tournament:
126 Grant Fox (NZL) in 1987

Above: Wales' George North, at 19, is the youngest try-scorer in Rugby World Cup history.

Above: Dan Carter kicks one of his two conversions for New Zealand against South Africa during their Rugby World Cup semi-final in 2015.

Most penalties:
58   Jonny Wilkinson (ENG)

Most successful penalties in a match:
8   Matt Burke (AUS) v South Africa, 1999
    Gavin I lastings (SCO) v Tonga, 1995
    Gonzalo Quesada (ARG) v Samoa, 1999
    Thierry Lacroix (FRA) v Ireland, 1995

Most penalties in a tournament:
31   Gonzalo Quesada (ARG) in 1991

Most conversions:
58   Dan Carter (NZL)

Most conversions in a match:
20   Simon Culhane (NZL) v Japan, 1995

Most conversions in a tournament:
30   Grant Fox (NZL) in 1987

Most drop goals:
14   Jonny Wilkinson (ENG)

Most drop goals in a match:
5   Jannie de Beer (RSA) against
    England in 1999

Most drop goals in a tournament:
8   Jonny Wilkinson (ENG) in 2003

Leading points-scorers by tournament:
Year, points, player (country)

Year	Points	Player (country)
1987	126	Grant Fox (NZL)
1991	68	Ralph Keyes (IRE)
1995	112	Thierry Lacroix (FRA)
1999	102	Gonzalo Quesada (ARG)
2003	113	Jonny Wilkinson (ENG)
2007	105	Percy Montgomery (RSA)
2011	62	Morné Steyn (RSA)
2015	97	Nicolás Sánchez (ARG)

APPEARANCE RECORDS

Most appearances:
Position, appearances, player (country, span)

1.   22   Jason Leonard (ENG, 1991-2003)
=   22   Richie McCaw (NZL, 2003-15)
3.   20   Schalk Burger (RSA, 2003-15)
=   20   George Gregan (AUS, 1995-2007)
=   20   Keven Mealamu (NZL, 2003-15)
6.   19   Mike Catt (ENG, 1995-2007)
=   19   Jonny Wilkinson (ENG, 1999-2011)
8.   18   Bryan Habana (RSA, 2007-15)
=   18   Raphaël Ibañez (FRA, 1999-2007)
=   18   Gethin Jenkins (WAL, 2003-15)
=   18   Martin Johnson (ENG, 1995-2003)
=   18   Mario Ledesma (ARG, 1999-2011)
=   18   Brian Lima (SAM, 1991-2007)
=   18   Victor Matfield (RSA, 2003-15)
=   18   Lewis Moody (ENG, 2003-11)

Oldest player:
Diego Ormaechea (URU) was 40 years and 26 days old when he played against South Africa in 1999.

Youngest player:
Vasil Lobzhanidze (GEO) was 18 years and 340 days old when he played against Tonga in 2015.

Youngest player in the final:
Jonah Lomu (NZL) was 20 years and 43 days old when he played against South Africa in the 1995 final.

Youngest Rugby World Cup winner:
François Steyn (RSA) was 20 years and 159 days old when South Africa won the tournament in 2007.

RWC 2019
TOURNAMENT CHART

POOL A

IRELAND
SCOTLAND
JAPAN
RUSSIA
SAMOA

POOL B

NEW ZEALAND
SOUTH AFRICA
ITALY
NAMIBIA
CANADA

POOL C

ENGLAND
FRANCE
ARGENTINA
USA
TONGA

POOL D

AUSTRALIA
WALES
GEORGIA
FIJI
URUGUAY

POOL A

20 Sep – Tokyo Stadium
JAPAN v RUSSIA

22 Sep – International Stadium Yokohama
IRELAND v SCOTLAND

24 Sep – Kumagaya Rugby Stadium
RUSSIA v SAMOA

28 Sep – Shizuoka Stadium Ecopa
JAPAN v IRELAND

30 Sep – Kobe Misaki Stadium
SCOTLAND v SAMOA

3 Oct – Kobe Misaki Stadium
IRELAND v RUSSIA

5 Oct – City of Toyota Stadium
JAPAN v SAMOA

9 Oct – Shizuoka Stadium Ecopa
SCOTLAND v RUSSIA

12 Oct – Fukuoka Hakatanomori Stadium
IRELAND v SAMOA

13 Oct – International Stadium Yokohama
JAPAN v SCOTLAND

POOL B

21 Sep – International Stadium Yokohama
NEW ZEALAND v SOUTH AFRICA

22 Sep – Hanazono Rugby Stadium
ITALY v NAMIBIA

26 Sep – Fukuoka Hakatanomori Stadium
ITALY v CANADA

28 Sep – City of Toyota Stadium
SOUTH AFRICA v NAMIBIA

2 Oct – Oita Stadium
NEW ZEALAND v CANADA

4 Oct – Shizuoka Stadium Ecopa
SOUTH AFRICA v ITALY

6 Oct – Tokyo Stadium
NEW ZEALAND v NAMIBIA

8 Oct – Kobe Misaki Stadium
SOUTH AFRICA v CANADA

12 Oct – City of Toyota Stadium
NEW ZEALAND v ITALY

13 Oct – Kamaishi Recovery Memorial Stadium
NAMIBIA v CANADA

POOL C

21 Sep – Tokyo Stadium
FRANCE v ARGENTINA

22 Sep – Sapporo Dome
ENGLAND v TONGA

26 Sep – Kobe Misaki Stadium
ENGLAND v USA

28 Sep – Hanazono Rugby Stadium
ARGENTINA v TONGA

2 Oct – Fukuoka Hakatanomori Stadium
FRANCE v USA

5 Oct – Tokyo Stadium
ENGLAND v ARGENTINA

6 Oct – Kumamoto Stadium
FRANCE v TONGA

9 Oct – Kumagaya Rugby Stadium
ARGENTINA v USA

12 Oct – International Stadium Yokohama
ENGLAND v FRANCE

13 Oct – Hanazono Rugby Stadium
USA v TONGA

POOL D

21 Sep – Sapporo Dome
AUSTRALIA v FIJI

23 Sep – City of Toyota Stadium
WALES v GEORGIA

25 Sep – Kamaishi Recovery Memorial Stadium
FIJI v URUGUAY

29 Sep – Kumagaya Rugby Stadium
GEORGIA v URUGUAY

29 Sep – Tokyo Stadium
AUSTRALIA v WALES

3 Oct – Hanazono Rugby Stadium
GEORGIA v FIJI

5 Oct – Oita Stadium
AUSTRALIA v URUGUAY

9 Oct – Oita Stadium
WALES v FIJI

11 Oct – Shizuoka Stadium Ecopa
AUSTRALIA v GEORGIA

13 Oct – Kumamoto Stadium
WALES v URUGUAY

QUARTER-FINAL 1	QUARTER-FINAL 2	QUARTER-FINAL 3	QUARTER-FINAL 4
19 October	19 October	20 October	20 October
OITA STADIUM	TOKYO STADIUM	OITA STADIUM	TOKYO STADIUM
WINNER POOL C	**WINNER POOL B**	**WINNER POOL D**	**WINNER POOL A**
V	V	V	V
RUNNER-UP POOL D	**RUNNER-UP POOL A**	**RUNNER-UP POOL C**	**RUNNER-UP POOL B**

SEMI-FINAL 1	SEMI-FINAL 2	BRONZE FINAL	FINAL
26 October	27 October	1 November	2 November
INTERNATIONAL STADIUM YOKOHAMA	INTERNATIONAL STADIUM YOKOHAMA	TOKYO STADIUM	INTERNATIONAL STADIUM YOKOHAMA
WINNER QUARTER-FINAL 1	**WINNER QUARTER-FINAL 3**	**LOSER SEMI-FINAL 1**	**WINNER SEMI-FINAL 1**
V	V	V	V
WINNER QUARTER-FINAL 2	**WINNER QUARTER-FINAL 4**	**LOSER SEMI-FINAL 2**	**WINNER SEMI-FINAL 2**

CREDITS